Dona Nobis Pacem

Grant Us Peace

By

Thomas K. Shannon

Published by Hemingway Publishers

Cover design by Hemingway Publishers

ISBN: Printed in the United States

TABLE OF CONTENTS

DEDICATION

To God, for Your grace and perfect timing. To Angela Shannon, for your constant love and encouragement, to Catherine Shannon, for the random calls to read me parts of the book, to Lindsey Windsor, for making growing older worth every minute, to Hannah and Thomas Windsor, for being the reason I took the publishing step. May I always have a place on your bookshelves.

ACKNOWLEDGMENT

I**t's** been a full life. Sometimes too full to allow for writing. From raising a child, building a marriage, focusing on a career, and enjoying time with friends, twenty-one years passed before I wrote "The End." Oh, but when I did write it, how great it felt to complete a personal quest! Thanks go out to everyone who crossed my path or who I bumped on the path, because so many things from my past were recalled to land on these pages. Even though she didn't remember when I asked, I told Julia Drost I'd acknowledge her because she inspired the bridge by losing her necklace a long time ago while walking with friends. God stepped in that night, as He does in this story.

THOMAS K. SHANNON

ABOUT THE AUTHOR

Tom Shannon resides in Maryland with his wife, Angela. He attended Immaculate Heart of Mary school, where his short story was read aloud by his second-grade teacher during class. It wasn't all that good, but it sure did make a memory. Tom also attended Loyola High School, now Loyola Blakefield, where he learned from the Jesuits how to critically think and become a young man. It was also at Loyola he found his life-long friends. After high school, Tom earned a degree in marketing from Loyola College, now Loyola University of Maryland. However, when his English professor scribed, "YOU CAN DO THIS!" at the top of a short story he had written, Tom immediately committed himself to somehow writing a novel.

THOMAS K. SHANNON

CHAPTER 1

Coach Max judged the shot's flight and determined it good a full quarter second before the crowd erupted in approval. He withstood the temptation to cheer as the ball went through the net. The job was not yet complete.

As the people in the stands rose in unison, arms raised and mouths stretched open, screaming unintelligible strains of joy, Peter was already watching the opponent's coach bring his hands together in the universal sign for "time out." He then shifted his focus to the court, hoping a referee or player from the other team would ensure it was called.

Davidsonville's assistant coaches created megaphones with their cupped hands and yelled "Time out!" toward no one in particular. At first, the deafening noise that filled the auditorium drowned out any attempt to be heard. Peter feared the ball would soon be put into play. He wanted that time-out called now.

Fortunately, after exiting the hoop, the ball had hit awkwardly in the mass of hands, heads, and shoulders tangled under the boards and rolled into the rows of fans lining the walls, causing the baseline ref to blow the ball dead and the clock to be stopped temporarily at eight seconds.

The interruption allowed one of the refs to glance over at Davidsonville's bench and take heed of the now red-faced coaches.

"Red time!" called the ref as he raised his right hand, which held the whistle, toward his mouth. Its shrill shriek overpowered the near-crazed screams of the crowd, bringing many of the fans back from their euphoric state. As the teams exited the court toward their respective benches, the noise had calmed, with only stray yelps and claps from high fives remaining from the eruption.

Peter Max approached the scorer's table and confirmed Davidsonville had just used their final time-out. Walking back, he went down on one knee into the space left clear for him and faced his team. He paused there, observing his team congratulating Danny Johnson on his go-ahead jumper.

"What's the score?" he asked.

His players reacted instantly, ending their conversations and turning towards their coach's voice. Hesitantly, Rob Thomas, the team captain, spoke up. "We're up one, Coach." he awkwardly responded, slightly confused by the question. Peter tilted his head and glanced at Rob. Nodding his head in short jerks, he covered his mouth with his hand and gently squeezed his upper lip between his thumb and forefinger as if trying to understand.

"How much time left, Danny?" he asked, through his hand. Danny Johnson's face came to attention as he raised his eyes toward the scoreboard. He knew the time was short but did not want to answer incorrectly.

Confident with his answer, Danny replied, "Eight seconds, Coach."

Peter again nodded, then looked down at the floor and paused. He silently counted to three, then lifted his head and scanned the eyes of each of his players.

The point had been made. The smiles were gone, and their eyes were fixed on him. The seated players were leaning toward him in anticipation, and the remaining players stood behind Peter, shoulder to shoulder, with hands-on knees and heads stretched forward. They were re-focused and ready to play.

"What play are they going to run?" he delved as his eyes again fixed on his Captain.

Quickly, the answer came back. "Stutter right, double back screen."

"Good...now, they're going to have to inbound the ball from the baseline, and they don't have any time outs. I want token

4

pressure...make sure they can't roll they ball up the floor to stop the clock from running. Once it's in play, fall back into half-court defense." Peter's speech was fast, but each word was crisp.

The cheerleaders had taken the floor, and as Peter spoke, the crowd regained momentum, and it began to scream collectively, in rhythmic voice, "DE-FENSE!!...DE-FENSE!!"

The noise grew, and the cheers once again became frenzied, but Peter's players never took their eyes off his. If the season had taught them anything, it was to trust their coach. Now was not the time to lose concentration.

It had been twelve years since the St. Francis Knights won a basketball championship. Peter Max accepted the varsity coach and history teacher position three years ago, and each year, his teams got progressively better. Some would say the success was due to intensity. Others would say talent, and still others, luck. Peter never denied or corrected anyone's opinion. He would simply acknowledge the conversation with a polite response, then quickly ask about an unrelated topic in the hope of changing the subject.

The noise did not affect Peter, either. He knew what he wanted to say, and he had gotten his players' attention. If the other team scored, it would not be because his team wasn't ready.

"O.K. look! We know Simpson is their first option to take the shot. Bill, you gotta get through the pick. If he catches the ball, do not foul. They are in the bonus.

If he catches the ball, we want him at least sixteen feet away. He'll have to hit that to win...understood?" Peter spoke directly to Bill Gibbons, but everyone nodded.

"When the ball is shot," Peter continued, "everyone must box out, get a body. Everyone! No tip-ins. When we get the rebound, hold it tight; no one takes it away. All right?" Again, everyone nodded. "Very important, we've got no time outs...no time outs...make sure you don't call one...understood?" Peter glanced at each starter to make sure they had gotten the message. Once again, heads were moving up and down. Peter waited. As one, they answered, "Got it."

Peter stood and momentarily turned away from the bench. He allowed himself to hear the cheers. Then, just as quickly, he turned them off again. He pulled his tie tight and adjusted the knot to the middle of his buttoned collar. As he turned to face his team, he smiled, and his eyes were wide with anticipation and pride.

He placed his right hand in the center of the huddle, and every player, assistant coach, and manager layered their hands on top.

"Gentlemen," Peter began, "you give me eight more seconds of solid ball, and I'll guarantee a feeling you will never forget. All right, let's go!"

With that, the huddle burst open with a guttural howl that seemingly propelled the players across the floor toward the half-court circle. Once there, the starters stared deliberately at the visitor's bench and waited for Davidsonville's huddle to break up.

Peter's attention was focused on the other team's huddle, as well. Their coach was kneeling, and although the gathering was guarded against a complete view, it was obvious the players were looking at the floor in front of their coach as he pointed to a clipboard. Something was up. The play Davidsonville had run all year, in close situations, did not require a diagram. His players had to know their roles by now.

They were going to run a different play.

Immediately, Peter's anticipation turned to panic, and he called for his center, Brad Taylor, and motioned him back to the bench. Just as he did, the horn blew, and the other team's huddle opened and as their battle cry erupted, the starters sprinted onto the court. Peter's arm began to move faster, and his center hurried to his side.

"Brad, when they run this play, your man escapes to the weak side, correct?" Brad nodded confirmation. "Okay. Look, I want you to leave him there, forget him. He is the last one they want shooting this shot. Instead, I want you to cheat to the play side, at the block." Before he could start another sentence, the refs blew the whistle to get Peter's attention. They wanted to start play.

Peter's index finger went up, and his arm extended toward the whistle. However, his eyes remained on Brad Taylor. He quickly uttered. "When Danny helps Bill get through his pick, I need you to get in front of Danny's man in the lane. If they find your man cross-court and can make that pass, so be it. In short, Brad, stop the extra pass! Understood?"

Peter's hand gently but firmly squeezed Brad's shoulder, and the center answered back, "I got it, Coach."

Brad Taylor jogged back to his position beside the opposing center just as the ball was handed to Davidsonville's guard downcourt. The remaining Davidsonville players lined up in a stack formation at the three-quarter court. The out-of-bounds guard slapped the ball, signaling the formation to explode in several directions.

As Coach Max had told them, the Knight's defense played loose, and the ball was passed to a Davidsonville guard near the baseline. Quickly, the Knights fell back into their half-court defense. The Davidsonville players raced into position, with two forwards lined vertically along the lower right side of the lane, and their center found a spot across the key as the point guard dribbled the ball low and fast at the hash mark, waiting for the play to take shape.

Scott Simpson, shooting guard, passed the half-court line on the left side of the floor as the clock read five seconds. Without breaking stride, he jabbed his lead foot toward the middle of the floor, then darted back around the first screen set by his center. Although Bill Gibbons knew the fake was coming, he had to protect the middle of the floor so that when Simpson made his swing around the first screen, he was already a step behind.

The first pick was a good one. Gibbons squarely collided with the Davidsonville center and had to roll toward the center of the key to release himself. After the spin, Gibbons found himself above Simpson, a full five feet away. Simpson scraped off the double-pick along the baseline. Gibbons knew he could not swing around the bottom pick in time to disrupt the pass or the shot. The best he could do was curve over the screens and hope to get a hand in Simpson's face, before he released the shot.

Three seconds. The St. Francis forwards reacted to Gibbons' problems by following Simpson toward the corner in the hope of delaying the pass from the point guard. The effort, however, proved too late as Simpson caught the pass chest high and turned toward the basket, fourteen feet from the rim.

Two seconds. As he faced the basket, Simpson knew he had a clear shot. He also knew his teammate was open at the blocks, having been abandoned by the charging St. Francis players.

The ball left his hands and arched over the frantically waving arms of the onrushing players. The Davidsonville forward watched as the ball approached his outstretched arms while his feet planted firmly to the floor in position to pivot toward the backboard. His hips shifted toward the basket, timing the flight, but as he brought his hands together to grasp the ball, his vision became blocked by a defender's arm reaching past his outside shoulder.

Brad Taylor's left hand intercepted the pass as he carefully contorted his body around the arched figure of the intended receiver.

The ball bounced lazily toward the sideline bench as the Davidsonville players collectively jerked their bodies forward in a hopeless effort to reach the loose ball and attempt any kind of shot. Instead, all they could do was watch the ball roll and wait for the inevitable buzzer.

As the final horn blew, the stands emptied onto the floor as if released from an invisible gate that had restrained them for the preceding forty minutes of play. Peter watched the crowd overcome his players, who gathered at the foul line in a joint embrace. He took note of their euphoric faces before the street-clothed throng of teenaged peers smothered them.

He then turned to his assistants and individually acknowledged each of them, accepting their congratulations and offering the same back. Once completed, Peter hid his smile and made his way toward the Davidsonville bench, pausing only momentarily to greet a student who had picked up the game ball. "One for the trophy case, Coach," he screamed as he gently presented the ball.

"To be sure...and thanks for watching out for it," Peter answered back, placing the ball under his arm and shaking the young man's hand.

He then turned toward the tap on his shoulder to find Walter Savage, Davidsonville's coach. "Congratulations, Peter... I was hoping to hold you off one more year."

"Thank you, Walt. It was a hell of a game. I have a feeling I'll be seeing you again soon."

"Yeah... next year... my place."

The two coaches shook hands, and Coach Savage slipped into the masses toward his locker room.

Upon Peter's earlier request, the custodian had left the scoreboard on, so when Peter exited his small office just off the gym floor, the score still shined. He had spent the last hour speaking first to his team about rewards and commitment, then to faculty members and the press, mainly about the return of school pride and the installment of spirit to an emotionless campus.

After thirty minutes, the questions had become repetitive and the verbal applause uncomfortable. Yet, he had prepared himself for the anguish and aggravation and, therefore, had spoken calmly and appreciatively until everyone was satisfied.

Now, he strolled to center court, carrying a pre-packed cooler and a portable speaker. As he moved, the red tinge from the scoreboard numbers fused through the darkness, providing just enough light to maneuver. He stood in the center court circle, placed the cooler directly on the school's logo, and removed his first victory beer.

The tab pulled back, and Peter was fascinated by how the simple sound of a beer being opened amplified in the empty gymnasium. He raised the can toward the rafters and stood motionless for several seconds, his eyes staring through the ceiling. With his thought complete, he tilted the can quickly and emptied a quarter of the can into his mouth.

"Piper, the last time I saw you with a beer on this campus, you were eighteen and had zits."

Peter jerked the can down and peered through the darkness as he wiped excess beer from his chin.

"The last time someone called me Piper," he paused and then replied toward the hidden voice, "I was a different person...the gym is closed, and I'm done answering questions. Now, if you'll excuse me, it's Miller time."

"Oh, you've changed your surroundings and directed your intensity toward different goals, but you're still the same as the last time I saw you. While the others were watching the boys play, I was watching you." The voice continued, "You can't bury who you are, Piper. You can only redirect it. Besides, if you are so different, why did I know you would spend your championship night alone in an empty gym?"

Peter took another extended drag from his can, then picked up the cooler and walked toward the home team stands. He placed the cooler on the first row of seats and, without turning, answered back, "This conversation is only twenty seconds old, and I'm already bored. Now, if you know anything about me, you will know when I start to get annoyed."

"Point taken." replied the still hidden voice. "I did know the first few seconds of our discussion might be awkward, but I never wanted to piss you off." Peter heard the dreadful sound of dress shoes walking on his basketball court as the now familiar voice moved closer. "Anyway, I was hoping you would have known me by now. I sure hope I don't have to remind you of my name."

Peter's face showed no emotion, but he was intrigued. Evidently, he was slow to realize the identity of the man approaching. While he wanted to know who it was, he really was not interested in being cordial to a forgotten friend from his teen

13

years. Prepared to make the best of the situation, Peter dried his wet hands from the iced can on his pants and rose to greet the visitor.

As he stood, watching and waiting, the approaching figure passed through the green backlighting of the "EXIT" sign over the Gym door, and Peter caught a glimpse of the man's silhouetted face. As if slapped by an unseen hand, Peter's head jerked back, and his shoulders straightened.

"Forgive me for not knowing your voice. I've heard a couple thousand tonight, many of them screaming," Peter spoke confidently and with a touch of sarcasm, "but I could never forget that nose."

"Again, you're no different from the last time I saw you. Anyway, it's nice to be remembered, no matter how demeaning it might be."

Peter took several steps forward to greet his friend. Peter Max and Steven Cross embraced spiritedly, even aggressively, as if a vibrant piece of their lives, long ago mutually extinguished, had just been rediscovered. After several moments, the embrace pushed back, with both men facing each other, hands on each other's shoulders, smiling, staring.

Before the moment could turn awkward and feel foolish, Peter spoke. "Beer?"

The left half of Steven's mouth cornered upward, and a breath of ease escaped his mouth. "What are you serving?" he playfully asked.

"Cold ones."

"That'll do."

The two men sat on the first row of stands, with the cooler between them. "What brings you back, Steven?" asked Peter after a short silence.

"The game, of course," answered Steven. "It's funny how things happen. Just a few days ago, I got the alumni email and, for whatever reason, clicked on it. And right there, jumping off the screen, I read where you were preparing for the championship after only three years on the job. I figured I'd wait 'til after the game so I could gauge what kind of mood you'd be in."

"I'm glad to know you still keep up with local events. I thought somehow that wouldn't interest you anymore." Peter opened the cooler and handed a can to Steven, then pulled another to replace his soon-to-be emptied first beer.

"You'd be surprised how often I think about my life here," replied Steven, gesturing into the blackness of the gym, "and you know, Piper, almost all of it is good. I thought tonight would be the right time to re-acquaint myself with some of the things I didn't want to leave behind."

Steven looked down at his finger as it traced the rim of his opened beer. He waited for some reply. When it didn't come, he pushed more words into the conversation. "And the night I choose to come back, I get to watch you give this school back its pride. I'll tell you, it was great! I was screaming as loud as anybody in this place...right into some old guy's ear too. He wasn't too happy about it after a while, so I told him to turn his hearing aid off if he didn't like it. I mean, Christ, he was at the State High School Championship game."

"Maybe he wanted Davidsonville to win," interjected Peter.

"All the better," Steven shot back. "I'm glad I pissed him off, then." The two men shared a laugh, then simultaneously drank from their cans. The laughing stuttered to a stop, and a few moments of topic searching began.

Finally, Peter broke the extended silence. "So, Steven," started Peter, "I've been hearing you're doing awfully well for yourself. Any truth to that?"

"You see, that's exactly why I'm here." Steven sat up straight, and his eyes grew wide. His voice became animated, with a sense of yearning. He reached over the cooler and placed his hand on Peter's forearm. "Eight years ago, we knew everything about each other. We could tell each other things we wouldn't have the guts to say in Confession. I could communicate with you with a glance or a gesture, you know?" Peter could see Steven looking through the darkness at him, and as he spoke, Peter heard the sincerity in his voice.

Steven continued, "Now, we struggle to say something interesting to each other, and we end up asking each other cocktail party questions within the first three minutes of a conversation."

"Come on, Steven, slow down. It has been eight years, you know. I'll need some time to settle into a comfortable conversation with you." Peter broke in on Steven's thoughts and attempted to bring their meeting back into what he believed was the proper context. "I mean, I'm really happy to see you, and I'm glad you came tonight, but let's not expect to re-create a friendship in three minutes that was forcibly halted for eight years." Peter was in tune with what Steven was saying, and his quick response made it evident this conversation had not taken Peter by surprise.

"Fair enough," Steven replied as he eased his hand back to the top of the cooler. "You know," he began, "you asked me what brought me back. The game tonight was the opportunity I've been waiting for to approach our friendship. I've done some very successful things with my life since I left, but I think it had more meaning to it eight years ago." He then lifted his beer to his mouth and, before drinking, asked Peter, "How's that for getting to the point?"

Peter shifted his weight forward and placed his right hand over his mouth. Slowly, he dragged his fingers past his lips, then down past his chin, as if in deep thought. Peter exhaled sharply and connected his eyes with Steven's, as he shifted his head inquisitively and asked, with confused interest, "Are you propositioning me?"

Peter could not mask his smile as Steven's face showed his embarrassment. Peter broke out in laughter, and Steven mockingly punched the air around Peter. His only response was a non-threatening but well-pronounced "Fuck You."

Two more beers followed, and the conversation grew less awkward and tense, in inverse proportion to the alcohol consumed.

Steven brought his empty can down onto the top of the cooler with a thud of finality and, without regard to the current conversation, quickly asked, "How 'bout some food...a little victory feast, if you will?"

"Thanks, but no," replied Peter, suddenly conscious that an hour and a half had passed. "Although I'm by myself, this night is dedicated to a couple of others."

Steven immediately comprehended and stood to leave. "Thanks for letting me intrude. Put in a good word for me. Hey, I'll be in town for a while. How 'bout we catch up while I'm here?"

"Sounds good. Where are you staying?" inquired Peter.

"I'm downtown at the Hyatt. Call me tomorrow, and we'll set something up." Steven Cross stepped forward and bent toward Peter, shaking his hand as Peter rose. "Hey, Piper, it was great to see you again."

"Likewise, Steven." The two men quickly man-hugged again, and Steven walked briskly toward the illuminated "EXIT" sign. Peter Max took hold of the cooler and speaker and climbed higher into the bleachers.

Outside, Steven opened his rental car door, and just before bowing into the driver's seat, he heard the distinctive sound of early Springsteen wailing from inside the gym.

He smiled as he thought to himself how some things just don't change.

CHAPTER 2

"r. Max, are you all right?" The rotund custodian placed a chubby hand on Peter's shoulder and gently rolled him back and forth on the bleacher. Again, he asked, "Coach Max, are you all right? Mr. Max?" Convinced the gentle approach had exhausted itself, the custodian placed both sizable hands on Peter's shoulders and bent his upper body forward, two feet off the bench, then let him drop.

The sudden jolt was enough to wake Peter, and his body tensed at the intrusion; quickly sitting up and searching with both arms for something to hold onto and regain his balance. It only took Peter a couple of seconds to realize two things: he had fallen asleep in the gym, and the sudden wakeup call had caused him to spill the remains of an open beer down the front of his shirt.

As he awkwardly brushed himself, He peered up at the smiling face of the large janitor and realized how enjoyable his act must have been to the rotund man. A small self-deprecating smile cracked Peter's lips.

"I am truly sorry to startle you, Coach Max, but this morning the Mother's club has reserved the gym, an' I just didn't think that was your best pose. And you know that Mrs. Flaherty with her camera always at the ready."

Peter winced at the thought of being caught in such a state. "Thanks, Jack," graveled Peter as he ran his hands through his unruly hair in a wasted attempt at straightening it.

The fat man sat down and rested his capsized shoes on the bench in front of him. "You know, from the floor, the way you were sprawled out, it almost looked like some of the Davidsonville faithful had gotten to you."

Peter contorted his body and reached both arms toward the ceiling, trying to work out some of the ill effects of bleacher sleeping. "Would you believe they snuck in last night and forcibly poured sixteen beers down my throat?" He lowered his arms and jestingly turned toward Jack, like a bad actor after a laugh. Somehow, the hangover and sore limbs had not diminished the joy from the night before.

"I'll stick with whatever you tell me," answered Jack. "You're the man."

Peter looked down at his wet shirt and viewed a mental picture of himself sleeping in the bleachers. He lowered his head into his hands and, between grunts of embarrassed laughter, asked, "Can you spell loser, Jack?"

"Sure can. D-A-V-I-D-S-O-N-V-I-L-L-E. And don't you forget it. So, you partied last night. In the three years I've known you, this is the first time I can count you in with the rest of us mistake-makin' humans around here. And believe me, a janitor knows a lot about the people who work here. You're the best there is, Coach Max."

As was usually the case, Peter shunned the compliment with a quick but earnest "thank you" and changed the subject. Although he was wearing a watch, he asked, "What time is it, Jack?"

"It is exactly 8:32."

"Shit...I should get rolling. You haven't picked up any stray shirts in your travels, have you, Jack?" inquired Peter. "I don't want to bump into Mrs. Flaherty smelling like this."

"Strays, no...but I have an extra I keep in my locker. It's an XXL, so that should work nicely. I'd offer my extra pants, but something tells me they might be slightly big on you."

"The shirt will be great. Thanks." Peter gratefully replied.

"I left my locker open this morning. Go ahead and help yourself, Coach. Return it whenever you get the chance."

"I'll have it back to you on Monday, Jack. Thanks a lot. I really appreciate it." Peter pushed himself off the bench using both arms and waited a few seconds to stabilize himself, before he slowly walked down the bleachers and toward the locker room. After walking several feet, he turned back and assumptively asked, "Oh, Jack, could you do me a favor and stow that speaker and cooler? I'll collect it Monday, as well."

"Sure thing, Coach Max. Consider it done."

"One more thing, Jack. How long have I known you?" Peter asked

"Well, we met the first day you came here, but I guess we've been talkin' seriously for the better part of two and a half years."

"Well then, either you're going to call me Peter, or I'm going to call you Mr. Jones."

"I ain't no Mr. Jones to you," protested Jack. "So, I'd be happy to call you Peter...or Piper. You might have forgotten I was also here when you were a student."

Peter stopped backpedaling and smiled. That name was part of a past he had chosen to forget. In his most polite voice, he responded, "No one calls me that anymore." He turned and entered the locker rooms.

==

It was 9:30 by the time Peter had groomed himself back to being presentable. He viewed Jack's shirt in the full-length mirror in the coach's office and acknowledged to himself that additional grooming was not going to help.

He stuffed his damp shirt into his duffel bag and zipped it shut. At his car, he placed the duffel bag in his trunk, then climbed into the driver's seat and, as a precaution, turned down the sound on the radio before rotating the ignition key. He exited the parking lot and proceeded toward the expressway. As was his routine, he was in the right lane, positioned to turn toward home.

Suddenly, as if on a dare, he jerked the car's steering wheel and maneuvered his way to the left ramp entrance. He merged into the light stream of Saturday morning traffic and headed toward the Hyatt Regency Hotel.

CHAPTER 3

The Hyatt was the first major hotel to open during the city's renaissance forty years earlier. For years, it enjoyed full occupancy and was the first choice for the city's promotional functions and conventions. The hotel stood thirty stories tall and covered the expanse of a full city block. The outside was mostly glass and had the kind of elevators that took its passengers outside the building for a panoramic view of the waterfront entertainment center.

It was not long after opening that the management learned that not all guests enjoyed the feeling of being exposed to nature. The situation was not aided by the experience of twelve diners who were caught between the 16th and 17th floors for two hours while riding the elevator to the rooftop restaurant. As luck would have it, a claustrophobic Mayor and a respected food critic for the local newspaper were included in the stranded capsule.

The next morning, the Hyatt began renovations on one of the three freight elevators for passenger use.

Peter drove his archaic blue Ford LTD into the driveway of the Hyatt and was late to notice the sign that read "Valet Parking only". Immediately, Peter searched his pockets for cash. While the car in front was being welcomed and escorted into the hotel, Peter arched his body from the seat and plunged both hands into his pants. He pulled out two crumpled one-dollar bills. He searched the pocket of Jack's shirt. Nothing!

The attendant waived him forward. Peter took his foot off the brake and let the car glide forward while he swept the week-old newspapers and convenience store coffee cups from his passenger seat to the floor in a wasted attempt at making the car more presentable.

The valet pulled open Peter's door as the car continued to drift forward. "Good morning, sir," he began. The car's momentum caused the attendant to walk with the vehicle as it progressed down the circular driveway. "Please place the car in park, and I will take care of everything." The sarcastic tone of the valet's voice was not lost on Peter.

Without a glance toward the young attendant, Peter responded by jerking the shift arm of the large car upward into a park, causing the wheels to lock and the car to lunge forward and then rock back. The tires chirped loudly on the pavement, causing several hotel guests and cabbies to focus their attention on the only visible person, the valet.

Once they identified the cause of the commotion, some hotel patrons snickered while others scoffed. All the valet could do was shrug his shoulders and offer a weak, humiliated smile.

Peter emerged from the car and stood close to the attendant, making the young man peer upward at his face. "I probably should have stopped before I did that, huh?" asked Peter, with a grin that warned against any further remark.

"That's perfectly all right, sir...that will be $12.00." The young man spoke quickly, having concluded he wanted this transaction to be over.

Peter placed his hand on the attendant's shoulder and firmly but non-threateningly positioned the teenager so they were again facing each other. Peter's face now showed a jovial quality.

"Look, do me favor, man." Peter gently squeezed the boy's shoulder as he grabbed his hand and exchanged the rolled-up dollar bills. He leaned closer to the young man's ear as if speaking in confidence. "I know you guys must keep a couple of spots open up here for VIP visitors. I'm only gonna be about fifteen minutes.... keep my car close, and I'll take care of you when I get back....OK?"

Peter continued to hold the attendant's hand to prevent him from seeing the value of the offering.

"I'm sorry, sir, we're just..."

"Twenty bucks."

"My pleasure, sir."

The doorman greeted Peter with a smile and a vibrant "Good Morning" as he pulled open the entrance to the hotel. Peter responded in kind as he passed.

The lobby of the Hyatt showed off its opulence with displays of yellow and white flowers arranged around the backdrop of burgundy and gold walls that towered four floors above the check-in desk, then opened into the cavernous setting of hallway railings, circling the entire height of the hotel. The floor tile and guest services area were marble, which distinctively captured the fluid sounds created by the three-story waterfall, which cascaded down into the fountain adjacent to the lobby bar.

The front desk clerk offered a smile and set himself to be of service as Peter approached.

"Welcome to the Hyatt Regency. How can I be of assistance, sir?" pitched the clerk. Peter smiled back. "Steven Cross' room, please," he replied. The clerk typed in the last name on his PC, and after verifying the room, he focused a more discerning look toward Peter. "Whom should I tell Mr. Cross is calling?" he inquired in a business tone.

Peter started to answer, then questioned, "Is that hotel policy?"

"It is a common policy for the type of accommodations afforded Mr. Cross...May I tell Mr. Cross who is calling, sir?" The question underlined the clerk's persistence.

The two men stared silently at one another for a moment while Peter reviewed the situation in his mind. "Is this a service Mr. Cross requested?" he curiously asked.

"It's merely something I like to offer our more prestigious customers. I assure you, it's nothing personal." The clerk finished his explanation with a cosmetic smile. Peter was about to offer his name when the clerk continued, "Of course, I would not expect that you would be aware of such amenities." The cosmetic smile now resembled a grin.

Peter leaned forward, placing both elbows on the desk, and looked directly at the clerk. Slowly, he spoke, "If he must know, tell him it's the guy he was hugging last night."

The clerk peered at Peter and waited for another response. None came. Visibly unnerved, the clerk dialed the number.

"Mr. Cross? This is William at the front desk...I am confident you had a pleasant night with us?.... Yes, sir, very well.... Mr. Cross, there is a gentleman here to see you.... No sir, he didn't say....yes sir,

I did ask him....he said....he said you were hugging him last night." The clerk spoke confidently, as if between friends. He waited smugly for the authority to dismiss the intruder. However, his confidence was quickly replaced by anxiety as the muffled voice on the telephone excitedly began speaking.

After several seconds of reply, the voice halted, and William the clerk, stared at Peter, then quickly looked away.

The agitated voice on the phone began again, and Peter could hear the voice coaxing William, "Go ahead and ask him." The clerk held his hand over the mouthpiece and said, "Mr. Cross wants to know if you brought your partner with you?"

With his elbows still on the desk's surface, Peter now rested his chin in his hands and whimsically looked at the clerk as he offered his answer. "You'll have to tell Mr. Cross that Cedric and I quarreled this morning, but I will more than makeup for his absence." As William placed the receiver to his mouth, Peter rocked forward interested to hear the response. William leaned back as Peter leaned in, pressing his back to the wall of the check-in area.

William, the now anxious clerk, looked toward the floor, removed his hand from the mouthpiece, and replied, "He said he is by himself." Again, the muffled voice was coaching William. The clerk was listening and shooting quick, embarrassed glances at Peter. Finally, he cut in. "Mr. Cross, perhaps it would be better if I put the gentleman on the line, and the two of you could work through your concerns."

Peter caught his smile as the voice on the telephone became faster and more excited. William, in turn, began gesturing toward the receiver, in an attempt to lower the voice of Mr. Cross.

After several seconds of listening, William replied, "Yes sir, I am here to be of assistance to you.... No, sir, I don't believe I agitated the gentleman... No sir, I was very polite to the gentlemen... Yes, sir, I am sure he is very good at what he does... No sir, it is not a problem for me to ask him that." The clerk again covered the mouthpiece and spent a moment gathering himself.

"Mr. Cross remains interested in your company. However, he wants me to inform you that he cannot pay the full fee if Cedric is not participating...Is that arrangement acceptable?" William, the now defeated clerk, offered meekly. His face was pleading with Peter to let him escape any further involvement.

Peter put both hands over his face and slowly moved them down from his forehead to his chin, pulling his skin as he went. Finally, in exasperation, he exhaled loudly and, with tired acceptance, replied, "Tell Mr. Cross it's a deal."

"The gentleman is on his way up, sir." William quickly replaced the receiver and handed Peter an access card. "Mr. Cross is staying in P-2. You will need this card for the elevator."

Peter accepted the card graciously and smiled broadly. As he turned to leave, Peter pulled four yellow flowers from the vase on the desk and asked William, "Do you mind?"

"Not at all, sir...please help yourself."

Peter nodded and walked briskly toward the elevator.

As Peter entered the capsule, he noticed a man dressed casually with a convenience store bag of groceries approaching the elevator as well. He pushed and held the "door open" button and waited for the middle-aged man to enter. "Much appreciated," he said, smiling gratefully, as he slid through the entrance. "No problem," Peter replied, returning the smile.

The elevator lurched upward and soon offered a grand view of the growing city skyline. Peter noticed his companion was facing the front of the elevator, his eyes shut, and his left arm tightly grasping the bag of groceries. His right shoulder leaned heavily against the side wall of the elevator, and each time the bell tone signaled another floor, the man's lips would silently mouth the floor number.

Peter watched this display for four bell tones before glancing at the elevator panel and seeing the number "20" illuminated. "You know," he began gently so as not to startle the man, "this hotel has an inside elevator. You don't have to see outside. Its location is marked on each floor."

"I know." admitted the man in a hushed voice, "But my wife loves the view, so I'm trying to get used to the ride."

"Are you on vacation?" Peter quickly replied, not wanting to explore the logic of being terrified for no good reason.

"Yeah...long weekend," forced the nervous gentleman.

"Just you and your wife?" Peter wanted to keep him occupied.

"And my daughter." The 20th bell tone sounded, and the man struggled through the opening doors of the elevator, bouncing off each side before staggering into the hallway.

A heavy sigh escaped the man's lips and his eyes opened again as the smile returned to his face.

"Oh, hey, before you go," said Peter, as his left arm caused the closing doors to retreat, "two each for your wife and daughter." Peter's right arm brought forth the yellow flowers and placed them inside the paper bag.

"Much appreciated." offered the man as the doors once again closed.

The elevator doors opened on the penthouse level, and as soon as Peter entered the hallway, he realized why the desk clerk had been so smug.

Hardwood floors stained a deep brown and adorned with floral rugs ran the length of the corridor. Mahogany tables were positioned every thirty feet with fresh floral arrangements, which highlighted the colors of the rug directly in front of them. The lighting was soft, and the walls displayed tasteful replicas of legendary artists. Under the frames were small gold-plated information plaques which told of the master and the time period of the painting.

As Peter walked, he made mental guesses at the identity of the artist, then read the plaque to see if he was correct. He arrived at the door to P-2 with a score of 2 out of 8, which was misleading since the Picasso was easy, and on every other picture, he had just guessed "Rembrandt" and got lucky once.

It was when Peter lifted his clenched hand to knock on the door he realized it was ajar. Glancing down to the floor, he saw a large champagne bottle wedged in the doorway, with the opened end facing out. Inside the neck of the bottle was a rolled piece of paper that had obviously been placed as a note. Peter replaced the bottle with his foot and read the message. *"Piper, get comfortable. I'm in the shower. S."*

Peter entered the foyer of the suite and placed the empty bottle on the Baby Grand piano as he passed. He suddenly felt awkward. He had heard Steven was doing well financially, but the room laid out in front of him spoke of "fuck you" money. The awkwardness, however, did not come from his being in such an impressive hotel suite. It was caused by his not being aware of just how well Steven must be doing. It had not been long ago when Peter knew all there was to know of his best friend.

Now, as he wandered in the openness of the hotel suite, he struggled for a start to a conversation with this same person. It is possible, maybe even expected, he thought, that eight years had changed who they each were. Certainly, he had spent the better part of that time reshaping his life. He had no other choice.

Likewise, Steven must have felt the same desire to erase the past and begin anew. After all, that was the reason he left town. It was also the reason they had not kept in touch.

Peter's tour ended at the living area's couch. He positioned himself at one end, with all but his shoes on the cushions. Several more minutes passed. Finally, on the brink of sleep, Peter found it necessary to sit up and inspect the crystal vase on the glass coffee table in front of the sofa. As he expected, it was Waterford.

The vase rolled between his hands as Peter became increasingly anxious. The rolling became tossing, and then, as a means to pass some time, Peter began throwing the vase as close as possible to the 13 ft. ceiling without hitting it.

After four attempts, he was in rhythm. The vase rose quickly from his hands and peaked within a couple of inches before plummeting into his waiting hands. On his twelfth release, Peter's eyes once again moved upward with the flight of the crystal. This time, however, they abruptly halted on the naked woman gliding across the carpet twenty feet in front of him.

The profiled view allowed for verification of all the best measurements. Peter opened his mouth and truly wanted to vocalize his presence. However, he fell silent as the women, reached the wet bar refrigerator and bent at the waist to investigate its contents.

Two things happened when the vase crashed through the glass coffee table. She frantically screamed, turned, lost her balance, and ended up on the floor with her legs spread and her back against the refrigerator door. Peter didn't move.

She crawled quickly behind the bar while Peter picked up the vase and inspected it for damage. "That's amazing," he observed, "not a scratch on it." He placed it on the metal framed edge of the splintered table and glanced toward the bar.

"I am really very sorry for startling you," Peter began. "You weren't what I expected to see. Didn't he tell you I was here?"

Her head appeared above the bar's surface, and for the first time, Peter realized how pretty she was.

"No, he did not," she replied with mortified anger. "Jimmy just asked me if I would get him some orange juice. He didn't say nothin' about me being on parade."

"Jimmy asked you, huh?" Peter rhetorically asked. "He must

have forgotten I was coming, I guess. Anyway, I'll close my eyes so you can head on back." After several moments, Peter heard her scamper toward the bedroom and closed the door with emphasis.

It was not long before she reappeared, still buttoning her blouse, purposefully heading toward the door. She stopped in the foyer and turned toward Peter, who was carefully gathering the largest pieces of glass.

She spoke quickly, "I don't think that was funny at all!"

"I agree it was unfortunate, and I apologize again for startling you, but I can assure you, I never once thought about laughing." Peter glanced up from his kneeling position and continued, "You are a pretty woman, and although I had no idea it was coming, the episode certainly left me with no regrets." Peter smiled at her when he finished, hoping to divert her anger.

She stood rigid, with her front leg bent and her back leg stiff. Her hands were placed on her hips, and her head was still tilted from when she last spoke. She locked her eyes on his, as if taking aim, and enunciated every letter in the word "Pig." She whirled on her heel and triumphantly exited with emphasis once again.

On cue, Steven entered the living area, dressed in pressed khakis and a button-down. He leaned against the doorway, crossed his legs and arms, and motioned with his eyes toward the freshly slammed door. "So, what did you think?" he questioned, looking for a grade.

Peter stopped piling the pieces of glass and sat back on the sofa. "About what?" he nonchalantly asked.

"Not bad for my first night back, huh?" Steven walked toward the refrigerator and replaced the unopened orange juice.

"She could do better," replied Peter indifferently. "In fact, I'm sure she has, many times."

Steven smirked while his right hand swatted away the friendly insult. He pulled a bar stool and partially sat with his feet still touching the floor and studied Peter. Several moments passed as the two men sat and looked at each other. Strangely, Peter did not feel nervous anymore.

Steven Cross's face was familiar to him. The time apart had not separated the ease he felt in the presence of his friend.

All the conversation starters Peter had rehearsed were suddenly swept away and rendered void by the simple silent greeting of Steven's gaze.

"So," Steven began, "how is Missy?" After he finished, Steven realized he might be progressing too swiftly. He squirmed a bit on the stool edge, then gathered himself and added, "I'm assuming that is who you dedicated last night's victory to."

Peter absorbed the question in the manner intended. "I don't know...she hasn't answered me yet. I do all the talking. If she does say something, I'm sure it will be to remind you she preferred 'Melissa.'"

"Yes, she probably would. Sometimes, I could drive her nuts by calling her that in public. I remember that night in line at the movies, she chased me around the whole building, swinging her purse until I finally apologized. You know, deep down, I think she really liked it when I did that to her." Steven leaned forward and waited for a confirming nod.

"No, she pretty much thought you were a dick when you did that," revealed Peter.

"Oh. I never knew."

Peter mused, "Maybe you should have paid more attention when she would chase you and yell, "Steven, stop being such a dick!"

The two men laughed as Peter rose and went to the suite window and drew open the curtains, revealing a splendid view of the harbor and shopping district with skyscrapers rising behind.

Peter turned his body 180 degrees, with his right arm outstretched and his index finger pointing to the plush surroundings, until he stopped at Steven and said, "Explain."

"Over lunch," came the reply. "Come on, you have to show

me how the city has changed in the eight years I've been gone."

Steven headed toward the door, and Peter followed. As Steven reached for the knob, Peter offered, "Hey, I'm sorry about the coffee table."

"Not a problem...worth every penny."

As the two men exited and Steven pulled the door shut, Peter inquired, "Do you have twenty bucks I can borrow?"

CHAPTER 4

The late morning sun forced its way through the dust-frosted front window of Shanhill's pub, providing the only light source. The front door was propped open to allow the stale air from the previous night to escape and mingle with the city's version of fresh air.

As the bar maid robotically wiped the beer-stained bar, she could see two heads bobbing along the curtain rod that cut the window in two.

As Steven and Peter passed the doorway, Steven darted into the dimly lit bar and halted his movement just as quickly, allowing his eyes to adjust to the blinding contrast. As he stood motionless, he could still hear Peter explaining the landlord's financial troubles caused by the building directly in front of them. Steven remained silent and listened as Peter's volume continued to ebb.

He smiled and breathed deeply when the voice abruptly stopped mid-sentence. Steven proceeded across the floor and seated himself two-thirds of the way into the empty bar. "There will be two of us." He exhaled as his weight thudded against the stool in feigned exhaustion. "...In about twelve seconds."

Peter rounded the opened door and firmly planted both feet inside the bar. Before his eyes could adjust to the darkness, he continued, "They've laid off over 120 people already, and the building is still only 40% capacity...you piece of shit."

The bar maid chuckled, and Steven confirmed his presence by offering a chair to his friend with his left foot.

Peter slid into the seat. "I'm guessing this is lunch."

"It's the alternative to hearing you talk business."

"I haven't talked business in four years. I talk businessman. There's a difference."

"Not when the person you're talking to doesn't give a shit."

Peter searched for a response, then acknowledged the remark by simply saying, "True enough." He raised an imaginary glass to toast his graciousness under the guise of defeat.

The bar maid approached with the bleach-soaked rag draped over her right shoulder and a beer in each hand. "Technically, we're not open 'til eleven on Saturdays, which only means I can't charge you for another 15 minutes." She placed the bottles in front of them and turned. "Besides, toasts work better with real drinks."

She was addressing them over her shoulder as she walked. Peter snatched the bottle in front of him and raised it toward her. "True enough," he agreeably offered as the bottle met his lips. She smiled back in genuine amusement. Peter smothered a wince as the taste of beer quickly reminded him of his escapade the night before.

"I landed in Connecticut," Steven began.

Peter's eyes focused from behind the tilted bottle. After another small sip, he rested the beer on the table and leaned in toward his friend. He wanted to hear every word.

Steven continued, "I don't know why I stopped there. I guess I figured a lot of rich New Yorkers lived there, and maybe I could get my hands on some of it without actually having to work in the city. Anyway, whatever the reason, I stopped at this upscale bar and restaurant and took a job as a bartender. Strictly temporary, ya know. I wasn't close to being in the mood to go back to a professional career, and I needed the money. So, there I was, almost thirty and wearing black polyester."

He stopped long enough to smirk and take a drink, then started again. Peter drank when he drank and listened while Steven spoke. "Not even good shifts. I mean, I had Sunday through Wednesday nights. I wasn't exactly raking it in. But after a while, when the bar never gets crowded, you start to recognize the people who come in, the regulars, you know. Most of 'em are losers. Some would be

44

waiting in their cars for me to open the place on Monday. But some of them would come in to talk. They were the ones who would order a drink and sip it for two hours while you listened. After the two hours, I'd ring them up for $11.00, and they'd leave me a fifty. Typical bartender stuff, I suppose."

Steven stopped again, and both men drank. Steven took a deep breath and went on. "Now…the interesting part. Alfred Sumner was one of my regulars. He came in three days after I started and didn't come back for a month and a half. I remembered him because he ordered a Manhattan, and schmuck that I was, I had no idea how to make it. So, I remember running in the back and one of the waitresses telling me which bottles to grab and bring to her. I ran back and forth three times before I came out with the damn thing. I stared at him while he took the first sip, and he nodded in approval. Simple enough. But he ends up drinking five of them. After the third one, the waitress tells me to go to hell, and I end up making the last two. He never said a word. Anyway, he pays by credit card, and his name sticks in my head. A month and a half later, he comes walking back in, and I immediately recognize his paunch and droopy eyes. Before he gets to a seat, I greet him with, 'Hello, Mr. Sumner…. Manhattan?'"

"He's yours, right?" interjects Peter. Both men drink, and Steven nods as his head goes back. Without stopping his nod, Steven swallows and brings his body forward. "Yeah, he's mine. But still, good generic bartending, right? No big deal. But then instead of a month and a half, he comes back in two weeks, then a few days, then every other day for three weeks straight, and his questions get more involved like he's testing me or something."

"You mean intellectually?" inquired Peter.

"Not so much that as ethically," answered Steven.

"Uh oh..." Peter let his bottle droop below his lips, and his head shook from side to side.

"Exactly." Steven nodded. "Except I caught on quick enough to give the answers I thought he wanted to hear. It must've worked because he stayed late one night and said he wanted to discuss something with me. I remember thinking he must want to introduce me to his fugly daughter or something...so I was thinking up excuses when he starts in."

Steven pulled his chair closer to the bar, leaned forward and looked Peter in the eyes. "'Steven,' he starts, 'I'm sure you've noticed I've been in a lot lately. I'm fond of the drink, of course, but I've become fond of you.' So now I'm thinking it may not be his daughter he wants me to meet, ya know. Anyway, he says, 'I own a decent size office equipment dealership, you know, copiers and document solutions. Owned it for thirty years. Made a hell of a living. But technology is going too fast for me. Hell, I built the damn business on buying Joe Purchaser beers at the pub and signing orders at titty bars. Now, I'm supposed to call on the IT Director and provide solutions to his freakin' problems. Let him figure it out, for Christ's sake. Just give me the order, put the machine under service contract, and buy toner, O.K.?'

"I like this guy," interjected Peter.

"You're going to love him in a minute," Steven responded. "So, he drains his Manhattan and takes a deep breath. 'Look', he says, 'I've got three things to deal with. The first is technology, and the second is the pressure from my manufacturers wanting more salespeople on the street. Ya think dealers for major manufacturers work for themselves? No freakin' way!'

"He stopped talking for a second, so I asked him, 'What's the third thing?' The rest of the conversation goes like this: He says, 'I'm sixty-two years old. I don't have the energy or the burn to carry my company to the next level...I want you to do that.'"

"I'm a bartender."

"For the time being."

What's wrong with your current sales manager?"

"He's reached his ceiling."

"Family?"

"Divorced, no children."

"Why me?"

"You're smooth, you're smart, you know the industry...and sooner or later, you're going to stop being a bartender. Why shouldn't it be to come with me?"

"I know the industry? What makes you say that?"

"I overheard you smooth talkin' one of the waitresses one night. You commented that you were the number one rep in the nation for Xerox before you became a bartender. I called some connections. You were second. Number one was a guy named Peter Max. But I figure you collect more panties by saying you were first."

"There was only a forty-thousand-dollar difference between first and second."

"Forty-eight thousand." Peter corrected sarcastically. "You're right, I love this guy."

"So enough of Alfred Sumner," relayed Steven. "I took the job. It turns out he did have a nice operation going. But he was right. It needed energy. He paid me 75 grand plus 10% of the increased sales profit. He had accumulated a nice retirement nut, so he basically turned over his business account for my use. He wasn't so much concerned about going out of business as he was about not going out on top. I immediately started a direct mail and media campaign. As it turned out, a lot of the expense was co-opted by the manufacturers. He had twelve reps when I took over. After three months, I canned four and hired six. I was working eighty hours a week, but hell, I didn't care. I had nothing else to do. After nine months, things started to happen. The advertising kicked in, and the reps started producing big. I made 125 grand in my first year. Sumner raised my base to 125 grand. The second year, I added four more reps and total sales went up another 25%."

"I made two hundred grand. Even better, Sumner and I were getting along great. What's not to like, right? By the fourth year, we had 25 reps, as many service techs, an IT department, and a revamped customer call center. I was making 500 grand. My bonus at the end of year four was 25% ownership."

Steven stopped to hoist his bottle. Peter didn't move. He wanted to absorb every word.

Steven began again. "Year six. The manufacturers are kissing Sumner's ass, and I'm working about thirty-five hours a week, with ten of them on the golf course. One day, he walks into my office, closes the door, and, with a huge grin, says he's reached his finish line. His nest egg is bulging with money, and he's just been informed his company is the dealer of the year for our major manufacturer. In a meeting that took four minutes, he tells me he wants to sell me the business for its worth on the day I started."

"Holy shit," muttered Peter.

49

"That's what I said." Steven smiled through his raised bottle. "We signed the papers, he retired, and I had 'President' added to my business cards. He grew sick about eight months later. Six months ago, he died."

Steven paused and shrugged his shoulders. He exhaled and looked at the floor. After several seconds, he began again. "I was devastated. I couldn't stand going into the office. I couldn't stand saying the name of his company. I'd show up late and leave early. Then, I get a letter from his attorney, requesting my presence at the reading of his will. I go. It's me, his neighbor, and his housekeeper. His neighbor gets possession of the Japanese Maple that straddled their property line for twenty years. His housekeeper gets all the kitchenware, two years' severance, and the antique sofa she always hinted about. The bulk of his wealth is given to three charities. Finally, after reading most of the will, one of the last entries mentions me. In effect, it says, 'To Steven Cross, the man who accepted the challenge and made me as proud as if he were my own son, I forgive all outstanding payments on the purchase of my company. I hereby pass ownership, in its entirety, over to you. In gratitude for my generosity, you will listen to the following advice, and I pray you take up the next challenge: Before you leave this earth, experience life to the fullest and add meaning to your being... You figure it out.'"

"Holy shit," Peter muttered, copying his earlier response.

"That's exactly what I said," replied Steven. "Three months ago, I sold the company to one of the national big boys…for a lot more money."

"That's an awesome story," said Peter, sensing the story had ended. I'm really happy you made out so well. Not only financially, but it seems Alfred Sumner was a great influence in your life."

"Absolutely," Steven answered quickly. "That's why I'm here. I'm taking his advice.

Every time I think about when my life had the most meaning, you pop into my head. I want to include you in my experience."

"What experience?" questioned Peter.

"I'm going to live life to the fullest, and I want you there," invited Steven.

Peter straightened on his stool, then fell back against the support. A long breath of air escaped his lips, and he sat expressionless for several moments. Finally, he fixed his gaze on Steven and quizzed, "What if I'm already living a full life?"

"Then you can explain to me what it means," challenged Steven without hesitation.

"I would think there's more than one explanation for that term," deflected Peter.

"I agree. But I have a feeling there is one common

denominator, and recently, I've accumulated a lot of it."

"Money can't buy you happiness," Peter remarked in a whimsical tone. He grimaced after saying it. "Ouch. Inane comments like that take their toll." He smiled and waited a moment before adding, "On a more serious note, I feel like I've righted my path. My life is under my control. That's all I want. Hell, it was quite a fight reclaiming some kind of purpose. I'm not sure I'm up to searching for fullness at the moment."

It was Steven's turn to ponder. He sat silently and absorbed his friend's comments. He decided on the generic approach. "So, what are you saying?" he began. "Are you saying the idea of fun, sun, shade, surf, turf, beer, wine & women, with a hell of a guy like me doesn't interest you?"

Peter appreciated the approach but let it pass. "All I'm saying is my life is simple. I've sculpted it from the ashes we were both left with. I'm in control of what I do and what I say. I owe nothing to anyone, and I've come to appreciate the small wonders of nature and the innocent spirit of youth. I don't feel the need to complicate my life with a brief excursion in search of euphoria."

"Holy shit," deadpanned Steven. He raised his arms and gestured to the eavesdropping waitress for two more beers. "Piper, this isn't about you. It's about me. I came back in search of what I left eight years ago. I'm not interested in fucking up your life. I'm interested in making mine exceptional. I know you can add to my experience. Maybe I can offer you something in return. At the very least, I know you won't suffer by coming with me."

The waitress brought the bottles over and waited for Peter's reply.

"Where do you plan on going?" he asked.

"No idea."

"How long?"

"You'll be back in time for the start of school."

"I'll have to cancel my summer leagues and camps."

"You won't miss the income."

"I can't leave until the middle of June."

"Perfect. That gives me three months to wrap up the sale and hand over a clean shop."

The waitress clapped her hands, smiled broadly, and simply said, "I don't need to hear another fuckin' word all day. Have fun, gentlemen."

As she turned to walk away, Peter and Steven clinked their bottles together.

CHAPTER 5

Peter reclined his seat and was surprised to find his legs rising as his torso went back. He was sure he must be causing the person behind him a great deal of grief, so he quickly reset his seat to its original position and glanced around its edge.

His concern vanished when he saw the woman already reclined herself. Peter again faced forward and concluded this was only the beginning of the foreign things he would experience over the next several weeks. He grinned as he pushed the gray leather chair into its seemingly unfair position once again. First class, he thought to himself, summed up all that was good about capitalism.

His position still afforded a view of the ever-growing gap between the ground and himself. As he stared outside, his thoughts went back to the overnight package he received two weeks earlier.

It was three months since he accepted Steven's invitation, and he was having trouble remembering why. Still, he made arrangements for his assistants to run his camp and worked prematurely on scheduling the Fall and Winter sports leagues. Such was his faith in Steven's word. He didn't need to question its sincerity.

So, when he returned home from his school office two weeks ago to find the overnight package lying in the hall beside his door, he already had a good idea who had sent it. Gingerly, he had positioned his paperwork and Kung-Pao chicken in his left arm so he could retrieve the package and still have enough maneuverability to open his door.

As he bent at the knees, Peter first confirmed his name and then looked at the return address. The only thing written was "Seymour Hiney". That was enough.

He walked across the dimly lit room to the kitchen and lowered the contents of his arms onto the counter. Without hesitation, Peter took a knife from the rack and slit the top of the overnight envelope. Turning the envelope upside down, two items spilled onto the counter's granite surface.

The most noticeable was the sheet of paper printed with airline ticket information. He picked that up first. His eyes perused the boxes of information, gathering the important facts.

Departure: June 18 - 11:32 a.m. Destination: San Diego, California. There was no return flight information.

Peter picked up the second item. It was a handwritten note that simply read:

Pack light - I don't know what you should bring 'cause I don't know where we're going.

S.

When he boarded the plane on June 18th, the only luggage Peter brought was above him in the overhead compartment.

As he closed his eyes, he allowed himself to remember why he had accepted Steven's invitation.

CHAPTER 6

The plane settled down at 2:45 p.m. local time. Peter exited the gate and reviewed the people waiting. The first pass did not pick up Steven. His second attempt found a uniformed man holding a placard for "I. P. Daily."

Peter's face brightened, even though his head shook side-to-side over the continuation of Steven's childhood pranks. He approached the capped man and extended his hand. The older gentleman reciprocated and questioned, "Mr. Daily?"

"I.P., please."

"Very well, sir. Mr. Hiney has sent word he will meet you at the hotel. I have a car waiting. After we get your luggage from the claim area, we can proceed."

"No need for baggage claim..." Peter stalled as he searched for a name tag. *Henry.* "...Henry. This is it." Peter jerked the dangling bag upward.

Recognizing his slow service, Henry hurriedly reached for the bag. Peter pulled it back with a gesture of nonchalance. "No worries, Henry, I got it." Peter smiled and patted Henry lightly on the shoulder as they both turned toward the exit.

The limousine pulled into the circular driveway of the Hyatt Regency San Diego as the concierge rushed to the rear door. The smaller bellman was nudged out of the way by the burlier of the two. With a smirk, the larger bellman opened the rear door and waited and waited.

The passenger side front door opened in front of the smaller doorman, and Peter Max stepped out. He handed the young man his only bag and, gesturing toward the burly bellman, added, "Some guys have all the luck, huh?"

Turning his attention back to the limo, Peter leaned in and said, "Hey, Henry, thanks for the quick tour and local information. Hope I didn't impose in the front seat."

"I truly enjoyed it, I.P. Anytime."

Peter held back his smile and presented $50 to Henry. "Thank you, but no, sir. Mr. Hiney has taken care of me already."

"That's Hiney's problem. This is from me." Peter leaned in and focused on Henry with a counterfeit grimace. "Let's not make a scene, OK?"

Henry smiled genuinely and took the money. Peter retreated

and closed the door. The bellman escorted him to the main desk and then to his room.

Once inside, the doorman proceeded to the drawn curtains and flung them open, revealing a panoramic view of the city. Timing his delivery, he began, "You are very fortunate, sir. You have a corner suite. As a rule, they have the best views. Most of the room's features are self-explanatory, but I would like to go over a few things. The wet bar is located directly beside the refrigerator and is filled with the very best liquors and snacks. Please indulge in whatever you like. For your convenience, we have included an assortment of gourmet coffees and a bean grinder. We also have..."

Peter left the bellman to his speech and walked toward the bedroom to deposit his bag. As he approached, something caught his eye, and he slowed his pace, making sure he was in the correct room. On the bed were three men's suits, each having its own distinct style. One was navy, one black, and one pale blue. The dresser was adorned with an assortment of silk ties, bundled by color and design. Beside the bed were four pairs of shoes that matched the styles of the suits. Peter turned around, looking for what was missing. He spotted a half dozen shirts hanging in the closet.

Standing in the doorway, Peter finally noticed the note taped to the door. He yanked it down and read:

The latest fashion. You'll never look better.

Don't ask me how I knew your sizes.

Lobby @ 8:00.

S.

"Ah, I see you've found the bedroom." The bellman squeezed past Peter and continued, oblivious to the wardrobe. "You'll notice a grand view from this room as well..."

"I've seen all I need," interrupted Peter. The young man turned to see Peter leaning against the door and holding out a twenty-dollar bill. He exited with a polite "thank you" and assured Peter of his assistance in anything he needed during his stay.

A few hours later, Peter exited the elevator at 8:10 p.m. As he proceeded into the main lobby, people stopped in place and stared, conversations halted, and eyes looked over electronics to catch a glimpse. One child, around the age of six or seven, sprinted from Peter's path and latched onto the leg of his Father.

At the same time, Steven's interest in the magazine he was reading was interrupted by the sudden silence surrounding him. Leaving the latest sentence half-read, he raised his eyes to spy Peter walking toward him. He methodically closed the magazine, placed it on the table beside the half-empty glass of vodka, and awaited the punishment he knew was coming.

Peter's bare feet were noiseless on the marble floor. His arms were at right angles, carrying the entire wardrobe Steven had left for him. He maintained eye contact with Steven over the boxes of shoes he had wedged underneath his chin for support. Behind him, he could begin to hear the murmur of voices and the giggles of couples he had passed. However, the eruption of laughter was caused by the little boy, who had released his father's leg and pointed at Peter, exclaiming, "Daddy, that manth's in hiths underpants!"

"I know, son," came the matter-of-fact reply.

"Why, Daddy?"

"Because he's an idiot."

Peter felt the contrast of the plush carpet on his feet as he entered the lobby lounge. He and Steven never lost eye contact as he hovered above him and opened his arms, allowing the cloth cargo to drop onto Steven's lap.

He turned on his heel, announcing, "I'll be down in fifteen minutes."

He marched silently back toward the bank of elevators. The little boy again clenched his father's leg, and at least two people rushed to push the elevator button, assuring there would be no delay for Peter to make his escape.

The doors opened as Peter walked proudly by the helpful strangers. Once inside, he faced the mesmerized crowd, showing them where he had stored his room key.

==

Peter returned at 8:30 and proceeded across the marble floor. No one remained from the previous twenty minutes, and Peter was thankful. His eyes perused the sitting area as he walked, then glanced toward the check-in counter. His anonymity was short-lived when the pretty clerk behind the desk playfully interrupted her duties to lean back, cross her arms, and inspect his outfit. Peter acknowledged her enjoyment with a wave as she gave him a thumbs-up signal and spoke, "I'm a bit disappointed, but that's a much better look for you in public, Mr. Max." He continued across the marble and noticed how silent the rubber soles of his bucks were on the marble floor. He also noticed Steven had changed seats.

Steven heard Peter's name and cut his conversation short with the women to his right. He placed his full glass of vodka on the table in front of him and stood. He was relieved to see Peter dressed, though rather casually. He wore tan khakis and a light blue shirt underneath a navy sports coat. As Peter approached, Steven locked his eyes on the colorful tie which accented the outfit.

"Nice tie," he knowingly commented.

"Thank you. I couldn't stand the thought of throwing it all out. Besides I just couldn't carry another thing on my last visit."

"I suppose it's ok to wear a $150 tie with a $20 shirt," Steven said.

"I suppose you're the only one who'll notice. Anyway, I forgot to tell the concierge I needed a tie for my outfit."

"You actually had the concierge go shopping for you?" Steven asked.

"Absolutely...they did a fine job, don't you think? I can wear this anywhere," Peter replied.

Steven opened his mouth to provide a retort when a voice behind him interrupted, "I think it looks great!"

Peter bent around Steven and smiled at the young woman still sitting on the sofa. He straightened again and simply offered, "See?"

Steven rolled his eyes and moved slightly to the side. He motioned at the young lady and said, "Peter Max, I'd like you to meet Linda Simmons."

"Simpson."

"Simpson...She just got off work in the rooftop lounge and was kind enough to share some local hotspots with me."

Peter extended his hand over the coffee table. "It's a pleasure to meet you, Linda. I hope Steven took good notes."

"I did better than that," reported Steven. "Linda and a friend of hers will be joining us for dinner and a couple of drinks." Peter felt Steven's elbow gently nudge him as he continued to hold Linda's hand.

"Is that right?" Peter spoke through his smile. "Well, this certainly has the makings of a long night."

Linda mistook his comment for flirtation and quickly replied, "Only if your niiicce."

Peter blinked both eyes and retracted his arm. As he turned away, he shot a grimace at Steven, placed his arm around his shoulder, and spun. Now facing away from Linda, Peter huddled close with Steven in order to speak quietly. Before a single word could be shared, the two men focused on the figure coming toward them. In an instant, they knew it was Linda's friend.

She approached them from thirty feet, strutting across the marble floor, her heels announcing each step. She practiced walking. Each step was a calculated exercise of one foot being placed directly in front of the other as her hips swayed to the imaginary beat of a slow erotic rhythm. Her dark stockings caressed her calves and lower thighs to where her legs plugged into the black leather skirt. The white cotton shirt exited the leather and tapered its way upward, billowing softly and tightly at the fourth button. From there, it opened, revealing what would have been a subtle necklace on most people's chests but rested as a display on hers. Her face was held high as she walked, with her auburn hair pulled back and her blue eyes navigating her path.

Peter knew the moment was lost. Steven turned to him and announced, "You're with Linda."

Steven stepped forward and opened his arms, proclaiming, "This must be Jenny!"

"Gina," corrected Linda.

"Gina...I'm really looking forward to the two of us having dinner with Peter and Linda. I've got a cab waiting; shall we go?" Steven extended his arm toward Gina, and when she accepted, he gently patted her hand as they walked toward the revolving doors.

Peter stood motionless and watched Steven and Gina push through the doors and disappear. He glanced at his watch. It was 8:35. He had lost total control in less than five minutes.

"Pete...Pete?...Earth to Pete!" Linda was impatiently waiting. Without his consent, they were now a couple. He turned his head and concentrated on her appearance. For the first time, he noticed how pretty she was and how nice her outfit outlined her trim body. Ultimately, she became nude in his head. He had removed her clothes and had to acknowledge how attractive she truly was. Any man would find her inviting. Any man would be counting the hours until they could retire to his room. Any man would weigh each word spoken and be careful to flower her with just the right compliment at just the right time. Any man would not only picture her nude but take the next steps toward imagining her in different nude positions, performing several nude maneuvers.

He reminded himself he wasn't any man. She was dressed again, and he wasn't interested. In that instant, he found it reassuring, yet slightly disturbing, how easily those thoughts were shut down and rendered void.

Peter placed his hand on the small of her back and gently urged her toward the doors. After she had started, he followed close behind. As they reached the revolving doors and she timed her entrance into the turning panels, he declared, "I call shotgun."

Peter bent into the front seat of the taxi and quickly smiled at the driver, whose dark complexion and choice of clothing labeled him as being from south of the border. Testing the language barrier, Peter questioned, "The hotel concierge suggests Armory Park as the best place to view a sunrise. Would you agree?"

The driver turned and listened intently to Peter's question. The delay in his response caused Peter to prematurely lament what was going to be a silent cab ride. Shockingly, the driver answered, "I can't say I've seen too many sunrises. I usually get to bed around four, you know." He gestured around the cab as proof of what kept him awake. He continued, "You must be from the other coast, yes?"

Peter was intrigued. "Yes," he answered, curious.

"Alonso's," stated Gina, leaning forward against the back seat.

The cab exited the driveway and entered traffic. Peter continued to look at the driver. "What made you decide I was from the East Coast?" He asked.

"Pretty sunrises happen over the Atlantic. Gorgeous sunsets are what you see in San Diego," came the explanation.

Peter nodded at the logic and was amused at how quickly his misconception was exposed and dissolved. "Then I'll want to know where to go for the best sunset experience."

"Spiritually or commercially?" Asked the driver, looking straight ahead.

"I'll be here for at least the next couple of days. How about both?" Peter turned in his seat slightly, pleasantly intrigued by the start of this conversation.

As the driver listed his criteria for best experiencing the natural wonder, Peter's position also allowed him to take in the orchestrated plan being carried out in the back seat.

Steven had placed himself between the two women and was playfully guiding the conversation, coaxing responses from both. Peter knew the content of the conversation didn't matter; it was the flow and reaction that were most important.

Steven would begin by asking a general question. When either Gina or Linda responded, he would turn his head to face them and genuinely ask, "Why do you say that?" He would then wait for the response and, at the right time, place his hand on the speaker's arm, as a physical interjection and shift his attention to the other women while lightly touching her just above the knee. "I think that's an interesting way to look at it. What do you think, (insert name)?" He was now gently holding one's arm while touching the leg of the other.

The driver had finished his recommendations, and as if on cue, Steven jovially questioned him, "How long will it take us to get to the restaurant?"

"Alonso's is about ten minutes from where we are now," came the reply.

"Fabulous, I'm starving...How 'bout you two?" Peter could see him stealthily caressing both women as he asked. He also knew Steven had asked the question, not because he wanted to know how long it would take to get to the restaurant, he wanted to know how long he had to work his plan inside the cab. A ten-minute ride gave him eight minutes to maneuver.

Peter turned his full attention back to the driver and simply petitioned, "Let me know when we're a couple blocks away." The two men in front resumed their conversation, as Peter left Steven to his work.

Several minutes passed as the two conversations continued. The driver was explaining the different styles of architecture to Peter but finally halted, as the noise from the back seat prohibited him from speaking in a normal tone. The conversation had gradually gotten louder with intermixed laughter for several minutes.

"Alonso's is about two lights up," dutifully stated the driver.

Peter took his cue to peer into the back seat. As the cab pulled into Alonso's lot, Steven now had his arms around both women and was intermittently pulling each close in order to whisper secrets in their ear. This would cause the one to laugh hysterically while the other begged him to tell her what was so funny.

Peter could only think how glad he was it wasn't a twenty-minute ride.

The four of them slid from the cab, and Peter paid the driver. He turned and followed his three companions into the restaurant, still huddled together, sharing amusing secrets.

Their progress stopped abruptly once inside. It quickly became apparent Alonso's was a popular place. The line to register with the hostess was three parties deep, and the people waiting filled the entire lobby.

Steven swung around with his arms locked around the two women and faced Peter. The group then bent forward and formed a huddle.

"It's got to be at least a two-hour wait. How 'bout we find another place?"

"Ohhh noooo," whined Linda. "This is the hottest place in town. Let's just wait in the bar. What's a couple hours? We can eat the snacks to hold us over."

"Yeah, I can wait," approved Gina.

Steven peered across the huddle and questioned Peter with his eyes. Peter responded, "Why don't you just work some more of your magic? I'm sure you can make that two-hour wait disappear." He tauntingly smiled at Steven.

The two women chimed in. "Yeah, Stevie, why don't you just talk to them."

"I'm not even from around here. I never heard of this place until fifteen minutes ago!" defended Steven.

"The particulars don't matter. It's the general situation you have to negotiate," prodded Peter.

"I suppose you could get us in quicker than I could?" Steven challenged.

"I'll give it a go." accepted Peter. The huddle stood straight, and Peter continued, "You and Gina go in first and tell them a party of four. Linda and I will follow in a few minutes, make our own reservations, and then meet you in the bar."

"Ok, let me just think a minute." Steven released the women and paced a small circle while piecing together the perfect words to use in speaking with the Maitre D.

He paced for forty seconds when Gina whined, "Stevieeee, other people are cutting in front of uuussss!"

Steven snapped to attention and proclaimed confidently, "All right, let's go eat!" He grabbed Gina's hand and determinedly strode toward the entrance.

Peter and Linda waited a few feet from the door and peered through the glass as Steven was awarded his turn in line. They could see him casually petition the host and even coerce a pleasant chuckle from him. After the short conversation, Steven patted the Maitre D on the shoulder and started to walk past. Suddenly, he stopped at the man's side, commanded his attention once again, and initiated what had to be a monetary handshake. The Maitre D responded kindly and attentively, then routinely placed his hand into his pocket, as a matter of course, before greeting the next party in line.

Outside, Peter confirmed the obvious. "Well, considering he doesn't even know how much Steven gave him, I'd say money is not the time saver we're looking for."

"Just make sure you tell him how much you're giving him. That might work," suggested Linda.

Peter glanced her way and acknowledged her input with a simple "Possibly," then went back to his reflection. "Or, perhaps he needs another kind of motivation. Come on, let's give it a try." The two started toward the doors. "And Linda...?"

"Yeah."

"Please don't say anything to the Maître D, OK?"

"Fine. It's your stupid contest."

"Thanks." Peter reached for the handle and, while opening the door, turned to Linda and delivered the punch line. "...And then the ump kicks dirt back on him and says, 'Go in the clubhouse and clean your uniform, cause you're outta here!' Well, Manny couldn't believe it, he was so mad he couldn't see straight. So, he starts to walk away, but he only gets about ten feet when he thinks up this great line. He turns around, drops his bat and helmet, and yells back...Hey, how you doin' tonight." Peter greeted the Maitre D, who was looking down at his waiting list.

"Good evening. How may I help you?" Came the robotic reply. After crossing off several tables and tallying up guest totals, he raised his head and looked inquisitively at Peter.

"Yeah, we're gonna have a drink or two in the bar with a

couple of friends, but I heard the food's good here...so why don't you put me down for four...and if we still feel like eatin' when you call us, we'll eat, OK?" Peter half-smiled and looked past the man into the bar area as if to search for his friends.

This lack of focus was not lost on the host. He placed his pen on top of his pad, confident he wouldn't be writing a name, and peered at Peter, timing his response. Drolly, he began, "The wait is currently over two hours and fifteen minutes...perhaps you might have better luck..."

"Huh, what?" Peter interrupted both the host and his search as if he didn't expect the host to talk and looked quizzically at him. Peter reassured him, saying, "Oh, that's alright, boss, just let me know..." Peter and Linda started past the stand, and Peter patted the man on the shoulder. Again, looking into the bar, he stopped and called back, "Hey, maybe we can get you as our waiter! Thanks, man." Peter held up his right arm as if to wave but continued the motion into a finger gun and pointed at the Maitre D'. He turned to walk into the bar with his arm around Linda.

Peter walked with a presumptive rhythm into the bar and was happy to find it more subdued than he imagined. The people waiting for dinner were huddled at the cocktail tables and the music was more for atmosphere than volume. As he jaunted past the tables, his head moved from side to side, looking at each party. When he spotted Steven and Gina seated at the far end of the bar, he again made the wave-finger gun gesture, but this time ended it by raising his index finger as an indication he would right over.

He continued forward and pulled out the last stool at the bar, located close to the waitress service bar. He knew the bartender would frequent that area. He motioned for Linda to sit, and he squeezed diagonally next to her against the bar.

Satisfied she had stayed quiet long enough, Linda sarcastically gushed, "Well, that certainly went well. You didn't even give him your name."

Peter placed a pretzel in his mouth and said simply, "That was scene one."

A waitress arrived at the service bar and forcefully smacked her drink tray against the stained oak bar to announce her presence. Peter waited until the bartender was close enough to hear, then started, "...And then the ump kicks dirt back on him and says, 'Go in the clubhouse and clean your uniform, cause you're outta here!' Well, Manny couldn't believe it, he was so mad he couldn't see straight. So, he starts to walk away, but he only gets about ten feet when he thinks up this great line. He turns around, drops his bat and helmet, and yells back...Hey, how you doin' tonight? Can we get a Maker's rocks and a chardonnay?"

The bartender indicated he got the order as he passed. After the waitress left, he poured the drinks but paused to answer the bar phone before bringing them over. After a few moments, he looked at Peter and nodded his head while speaking into the receiver. He placed it on the counter and brought over the drinks.

"One Maker's rocks and a chardonnay...that's the Maitre D on the line....says he doesn't have a name for you."

Peter again looked up quizzically, then smiled and, while looking at Linda, said, "Man, this is refreshing...I forgot we weren't in LA. Sorry 'bout that, boss....Madson."

The bartender looked at him more intently after he gave his answer. He paused momentarily before going back to the phone. When he did, Peter noticed he again glanced back and seemingly provided more information than the name to Maitre D. Peter listened intently but could only make out the last few words of the conversation,

"I'm not positive, but I think it's him...ok, I'll try."

Peter looked at Linda and raised his eyebrows, waiting for her response.

"Who?" was all she could say.

Peter grinned as he began to leave her side. From behind, he placed his hands on her shoulders and whispered in her ear, "That was scene two...now for the climax."

As he walked toward the men's room, he could hear her say, "What are you talking about?"

Five minutes later, Peter again walked through the bar and positioned himself next to Linda. He glanced at his watch and commented, "It shouldn't be long now...We might do this in under fifteen minutes."

Linda took an extended drink from her wine and matter-of-factly stated, "I think you should just pay Stevie whatever you're gonna owe him and get it over with...I don't think we're eating anytime soon."

Another waitress announced her arrival at the service bar, and Peter watched as the bartender approached. When the bartender was within hearing distance, Peter was tapped on the shoulder by another customer.

"Excuse me, Mr. Madson...I'm a big fan...and so's my son....would you mind giving me your autograph?" While turning to face the inquirer, Peter noted the bartender's complete attention to the scene.

When he completed his turn, he was presented with a pen and cocktail napkin by a 40-year-old man with a huge smile.

"My pleasure...I didn't expect to get recognized out here... who should I make it out to?"

"Make it out to Bobby....Geez, he's not gonna believe it...We moved here from Philadelphia, and we hated to see you leave, but we never stopped following you. Boy, you had a great year with the Dodgers."

"Thanks, man...that means a lot....here you go." Peter handed him the pen and napkin and turned back to the bar. The fan went back to his seat, and Peter watched as the bartender approached him. After a short discussion, the fan proudly produced the napkin. The bartender held it under the register light and read, "To Bobby, always go with your fastball! Your friend, Ryan Madson."

After reading the note, he focused on Peter, who had taken an uncut lemon from the fruit tray and was showing Linda how to throw a curveball. Quickly, the bartender returned the napkin and picked up the phone. Peter looked past the lemon toward the Maitre D and watched him answer the ring.

He replaced the lemon, leaned into Linda, and asked, "Have you decided what you want to eat?"

He straightened and stood tall, searching for Steven. When the two made eye contact, Peter gestured for him to drink up and pointed toward the main restaurant. Steven waved him off and said something to Gina, but Peter repeated his gestures. Finally, Steven left his tip and led Gina down the bar.

Steven knew what he was going to say but never got the

chance. The Maitre D arrived with four menus and asked if they were ready to be seated. Steven could only rotate his stare between Peter and the Maitre D.

Peter acknowledged the Maitre D with a big smile, then looked at his three companions and questioned, "I don't know. Are you guys hungry yet?" After waiting for a response but not receiving one, he turned back to the Maitre D and said, "Yeah, I guess we're ready...Thanks, boss man."

"Very good, sir. I've got a special table ready for you."

The group filed behind Peter as they proceeded into the dining room. As they walked, Peter looked back at the fan and gave him his now signature wave/pistol signal. The man knowingly returned the gesture.

Peter caught up with the Maitre D' and inquired, "Hey, were you able to work out being our waiter?" He noticed the man's shoulders tighten as they exited the bar.

Upon the group's departure, and with the bartender otherwise occupied, the fan wiped up a beer spill with his autographed napkin and tossed it into the trash.

CHAPTER 7

A former athlete-turned-dad with a paunch awkwardly rolled by on his birthday present. The in-line skates were probably a reasonable request at the time. Now, standing in his boots with wheels for the first time, he pondered if there would be a second attempt at this awful exercise.

Peter watched the man extend his right leg and glide along the pavement, then pull it back and take an agonizingly small step with his left, simply because he had to if he wanted to keep rolling. Peter watched this for several more yards until the man pulled off the asphalt path to let a young couple pedal past. He remained stationary, waiting for a mother with her stroller to go by, as well. Satisfied the coast was clear, he spread his arms, climbed back on the smooth surface, and began the process again.

It had been six days since Peter arrived in San Diego. For the last four, he had ended his morning run at the reflecting pool in Balboa Park. From here, he could see the city come alive and start its day. The view from his bench allowed him to experience the city's personality. Each morning, the same asphalt path served as a venue for both vagrants and executives, adolescents trudging to school and middle-aged men clinging to their youth, young mothers strolling with their children, and career women already conducting business on their phones. The pleasant breeze would dry his sweat, and the early sun would illuminate the leaves, creating a backlit stage for each morning's show.

Alas, they were all merely part of the supporting cast. The reason Peter came back each day was to watch the unwitting command performance of the two main characters.

On the first morning, Peter had taken both the limo and cab driver's advice to visit the park, and he paused momentarily to look at the reflecting pool and the surrounding picnic area. After mentally checking the event off his mental to-do list, he turned to continue his run. It was then he noticed the playground just across the asphalt path.

It wasn't so much the park that interested him as to who was using it. A mother had arrived with her daughter. There was nothing unusual about the two, yet their presence compelled Peter to sit on the bench and consume their actions. After the first morning, he knew he would start each day on that bench and anxiously await their arrival.

At 8:42 they came over the small hill about a hundred yards

away, she on her tricycle and mom within protective distance. At eighty yards, Peter could see her face light up with the biggest smile she could muster as she first caught sight of the playground. She continued to pedal, turning her head toward her mother while pointing at the small spot of land and proclaiming, "Look, Mommy, there it is!" The force of her head turn caused her arms to pull the handlebars, and the tricycle veered sharply from one side of the path to the other.

The smile quickly disappeared as she went into corrective maneuvers. She again faced forward as her arms jerked the handlebars back too far, and the small bike swerved to the other bank. Totally involved in her predicament, the young girl was unaware she was still pedaling. Once again, she yanked the handlebars and the bike again responded by crossing the path. Her eyes were wide, and her tongue was pushed out so far it nearly touched her chin. Finally, in a last-ditch effort, the girl locked the brakes, and the tricycle came to a halt inches away from rolling off the two-inch drop onto the grass.

After thinking through her experience, the girl's face again brightened, and her mouth became wide with laughter.

The Mother had quickened her step, in case her reaction had differed, then, with an appreciation of the comedic moment, issued a delighted lesson. "Michelle, you have to pay attention when you ride your bike! Eyes straight ahead!" She had caught up with her and mussed her blond hair as she gently pushed her back and started her on her way.

They made it to the playground without further incident, and she impatiently waited as Mom removed her light jacket. She folded it and placed it alongside her bike as Michelle ran across the sand and climbed the ladder to the sliding board. By the time she reached the top, Mom was waiting at the bottom. She slid down into her arms and was lifted skyward as if she were on display.

After all, she was. Peter continued to watch as the girl moved from station to station, gleefully laughing with Mom one step behind, smiling. She was oblivious to everything else but her. She found exhilaration in her joy. Peter was captivated by the two-somes genuine interactions. He knew their display was meant for no one to see, yet the scene stirred such passion within him that he forgave himself for eavesdropping.

So enthralled was he in their routine, that he hadn't noticed Steven Cross sit down beside him.

"How old would Anna be now?" Steven asked.

Peter withdrew his focus from the playground and pressed his back against the bench. He looked at Steven and understood that he must have been there long enough to witness his infatuation. He also was aware that Steven knew the answer to his own question.

However, he could tell Steven was extending himself as a friend.

"Eleven," Peter glanced back at the playground, leaned forward again, and pointed with his chin at the mother and daughter. "They really know they are the only ones who count." After several seconds, he leaned back again and asked, "How did you know I'd be here?"

"I overheard the cab driver the first night we were in town tell you about this place...I took a shot. Plus, the doorman at the hotel said he sees you coming back from this direction every morning."

"9:00...isn't it a bit early for you?"

"She had to get up for work this morning, and I couldn't get back to sleep...I called your room, but you weren't there, so I came looking."

"Which she is that?"

"The one you turned down, but then that still doesn't clear things up, does it?" Steven asked, shook his head, and pointedly slapped Peter on the shoulder. "What's up with that anyway? At least three of the nights we've been here, you've blown off some very worthwhile lays...You cut it off or somethin'?"

Peter put the playground out of his view and answered flatly, "I just don't have any use for women anymore."

"Hell, I've only got one use for them."

Peter focused on Steven and observed, "Yeah, you seem to have gotten over Pam, or maybe not."

"I'm not sure what you mean, but it's evident you haven't gotten over Melissa," Steven had forced the issue, and he knew it.

When Peter didn't react, he continued, "Look, what happened took its toll on me, too. I couldn't even look at you, much less spend time with you afterward. That's why I had to leave town. You stayed, and I think that's great...but maybe you never got the chance to let it all go. You can't spend your life punishing yourself for what happened eight years ago. Melissa's not going to come back. You need to start experiencing life again. Look at me..."

"Yeah, look at you..." Peter cut him off, "...You go to the other extreme. I have no use for them; you just use them."

Steven and Peter were locked in on each other. This was the first time they allowed themselves to talk about the event that nearly destroyed them both. They sat on the bench and contemplated going further. They weren't angry; they were tentative. Each of them had gone their separate way and tried their best to cope with their losses. Now, having never before opened up to anyone, they were on the brink of either salvaging or demolishing their friendship.

Peter continued, "Look, Steven, I've got no use for women, not because I'd feel guilty about Melissa; I don't have any use for them because if I don't get intimate, I can't get hurt again."

85

He had never told anyone that before, and he wasn't quite sure how it sounded. He only knew that for the first two years after he lost his wife and daughter, he was reduced to counting the minutes and hours of each day. The sun simply came up every morning and plainly went down each night. Between the two, he survived.

He had thrown himself into his work and left his integrity behind. He no longer cared how he made his sales as long as he made them. His life was an act. He made it a play, and he was playing the part of a cutthroat salesman. He had always been a skilled salesperson, but he decided he would get meaning from his success. He would say what he needed to, stay out as long as he needed, subtly turn conversations around to further his career, bad mouth peers when convenient, and kiss ass when it meant money. His numbers soared, and he became the mentor for several new trainees.

Finally, on the first day of the New Year, Peter Max looked at himself in the mirror while shaving and immediately looked away. He forced himself to look again and acknowledge who he had become. For the first time since the accident, he collapsed in the corner of the bathroom, rolled up in the fetal position, and sobbed uncontrollably.

He never returned to work.

"I know what you went through, Peter." Steven wanted to continue but had to wait momentarily for Peter to regain his attention. Peter's eyes locked with his, yet he knew Peter was looking at something else. It only took an instant. Peter quickly blinked and slightly twitched before locking in again. Satisfied he was being heard, Steven proceeded, "Hell, when I lost Pam, I thought my head would explode. Nothing made sense, and nothing mattered. People would show me sympathy, and all I could do was offer some lame-ass response. I don't even know how many people I talked to after the news spread. I can't remember how I fed myself or if I showered the day of the funeral. The only thing I remember like it was yesterday was waking up one morning, about two months after the accident, in some alley on the West end. I didn't know how I got there or how long I was passed out. I just remember waking up with puke all down my shirt and realizing shortly after that I had shit and pissed myself. I tried to get up but fell right back on my ass. My head hurt so much. I reached up and felt a huge knot on my forehead. I can only guess I hit my head when I passed out the night before. I finally managed to stand up and literally had to hold the wall of the building as I staggered out of the alley onto the street. I could hardly see; it took me about ten minutes just to figure out where I was, man..." Steven's voice trailed off, and he lowered his head. Just as quickly, he raised it again, and his body tensed. When he spoke again, his voice was deeper, and his tone determined. "That was the 'rock bottom' everyone talks about. I decided then and there that I would never again allow a situation or event to dictate my response. Never again would anyone or anything cause me to lose control. I would make the terms, and I would draw the lines. If I didn't get pleasure from it, I wouldn't do it. End of story."

"It appears we both made the same vow to ourselves," observed Peter. "Perhaps the differences lie in what we deem pleasurable."

"You're not having fun?" questioned Steven. "Limo rides and hotel suites aren't your thing? Twenty-dollar cigars and center aisle seats just don't do it for you?" Steven's tone was now more sarcastic than serious. He knew the answers. Over the last six days, he had seen the smiles and heard his laughter.

"I've nothing against the things money buys," noted Peter quickly. "I absolutely love nice cars and fancy clothes. I can savor the taste of a '94 cabernet. But..." Peter raised his finger to dramatize his point, "...the money is not what is causing my pleasure. The way I experience our time together is what is pleasurable. I've smiled my way through a lot of two-dollar steaks and warm beer. I've danced to a ton of bad music and shed tears at the sappiest of songs - the memories are just as great." Peter paused.

Steven's expression displayed his acceptance.

Peter added, "I've come to know my best memories have been

created by just...*being there*." Pleased with his summation, Peter leaned back against the bench and folded his arms across his chest.

"I'll keep that in mind when I book you right above the nightclub, with a view of the parking lot, at our next hotel," offered Steven, still aware of some of the cards he held.

"Just as long as I don't have to give up my Jacuzzi," mused Peter.

"Oh no, Piper," shot back Steven. "You'll be lucky to get hot water."

Now, both men had their arms crossed and lazily gazed at the playground, long since abandoned.

Something Steven said finally registered with Peter. "Next hotel, huh? Does that mean we're moving on?"

"I guess so. I think we've gotten a good taste of San Diego, huh?"

"Where to?"

"Don't know yet. Any suggestions?"

"Makes no difference."

Steven suddenly decided the bench had served its purpose. He stood quickly and faced his friend. "Tell you what then, tonight we'll head over to Coronado Beach, watch the sunset, and let it come to us. Sound good?"

"Sounds like the plan," responded Peter, understanding the conversation was ending.

"Great! I've got lunch with Karen. Want to come?"

"Doesn't sound like a plan," Peter shot back.

"Ok, don't say I didn't ask. I'll meet you at 6:00, and we'll catch a cab," Steven turned and began to walk back toward the hotel. After several steps, he called back, "Piper...just you and me tonight."

"You must be getting tired," Peter remarked.

Steven disappeared over a hill, to be replaced by a guy walking toward him with orange-spiked hair, wearing a leather jacket, knee-length shorts, and construction boots. As he got closer, Peter could see the title of the book he carried at his side.

It read, "A Key to Shakespeare's Sonnets."

CHAPTER 8

The Sun glowed a subdued orange as it prepared for its scheduled demise. It descended royally, casting itself into the surrounding heavens, throwing forth its rays, and providing character to previously mundane clouds.

It exited gracefully, placing its signature on another successful shift. It left silently, yet brilliantly.

"Now that's what I call a perfect ass!" Steven exclaimed through his cigar-clenched teeth.

Peter heard his friend, of course, but chose to continue watching what had become a magnificent sunset. He was bent at the waist with his elbows resting on the railing, his arms extended toward the Pacific Ocean, with the Sun directly above the beer bottle in his hands.

He just needed a few more moments. He wanted to see the fire of the glowing orb meet the darkness of the water and dent its perfect circle.

"Piper, man, you're missing this ass!" Steven nudged his friend. Grudgingly, he turned to join Peter on the rail. Taking a long draw on his cigar, he exhaled a thick, odorous cloud of smoke, saying, "Son, you gotta get your priorities back in whack." He pointed toward the ocean. "I mean, that's pretty and all, but it happens every day. I had my sights on the kind of ass you only get to see every once in a while. Now that's a treat."

"Don't get me wrong, a nice ass is worth seeing," Peter pointed toward the ocean. "But just like every woman's ass is different, so is every sunset. Tonight's was not to be tampered with." Peter turned to face the crowd of people gathered on the deck, "Now, where is your discovery?"

"Too late, nature boy, she's sitting down. No tellin' when she may have to get up again."

"Oh well, my loss, I suppose," said Peter, feigning regret. "But, on the other hand, from what I've seen, your only criteria for a nice ass is that it has a crack going down the middle," Peter nudged his friend and gave a sarcastic wink.

"At least I know I won't have to compete with you for any companionship," noted Steven.

"You're welcome."

"Yeah, right."

"You know it."

Steven stared at Peter for a moment, contemplating what he should say. He could tell, by the way, he leaned against the rail and sipped his beer, Peter was prepared for a battle of words. He decided to file this challenge until the appropriate time.

Instead, he took a different angle. "Let's get some dinner; it's getting cold and dark out here," invited Steven.

Peter lowered his bottle and was mildly surprised at how easily his friend relented. Nonetheless, he was hungry, and the wind was starting to pick up. "Ok. I saw the menu when we came in, and it looked decent. I'll buy it tonight."

"Uh-oh," said Steven playfully. "Nothing over ten bucks, I'll bet."

"So that's what you think of me?" Peter commented. "I'll have you know there's plenty of overpriced food in here."

The two friends laughed as they walked from the deck and opened the door to the main restaurant. As they entered, Peter held Steven's shoulder and added, "But you only get to order from the left side of the menu."

"All right, then. Six shrimp cocktails for me." Steven raised his arm defiantly and marched toward the hostess stand.

They were seated immediately at a nice table near the window.

Peter glanced out at the ocean and could barely make out the faint remains of light on the horizon. They were only seated for a few seconds when Peter felt a tug on his sleeve. It was Steven, and he was jerking both his head and his eyes to the left while raising his eyebrows.

Although he wasn't making a sound, Steven created such a commotion with his antics the first thing Peter thought to say was, "SSHHHH."

Steven stopped but kept his eyebrows raised and slowly nodded his head in self-validation.

Peter followed the previous directions and looked past Steven to the left. He found the obvious discovery and seated two tables from them.

He smiled broadly at his friends' adolescents and turned back to Steven, whose eyebrows remained raised.

"Nice ass, right?" confirmed Peter.

"Yep."

Peter glanced over again. She certainly was attractive.

"I think she's alone," Steven whispered.

"No way," he responded. "Women like that don't eat alone. Besides, she's sitting at a table for four."

"Yeah, but she's got a plate of food in front of her with no one else there."

"Doesn't mean a thing."

"Watch and learn, Father Max." Steven chuckled at his crack on Peter, then approached the women's table. Without allowing her to object, he introduced himself and sat down at the same time. When she smiled knowingly but did not respond, Steven offered, "My friend and I couldn't help but notice you were eating by yourself."

"Oh, no," she began. But Steven was not finished with his lure.

"No, no, it's ok. I was just going to say we have room at our table, and we would love to have your company. Hell, we're here by ourselves, too. After dinner, we can go our separate ways. You've got nothing to worry about. My friend doesn't even like girls anymore."

Peter almost dropped his water glass on the table. He snapped his head over at Steven, who was having trouble keeping a straight face.

"Thank you, you're very sweet...and funny. But I am actually waiting for someone," objected the woman mildly.

"Really? Then why have you already started to eat?"

Questioned Steven.

"Because I was sitting here by myself, waiting, and I got hungry," she stated with slightly more force. "Besides, it's only an appetizer."

Steven lowered his head, acting deflated. He noticed she wasn't wearing a wedding ring. Still confident that Peter would be listening and not wanting to miss an opportunity, he probed, "Oh, I see. Well, is it your girlfriend? Because my friend doesn't actually hate women, he just has no use for them." He glanced up at Peter with that same grin but was rather perplexed to see him calmly drinking from his glass and watching. He raised his glass to his friend as if wishing him luck.

"No, dip shit, it's her boyfriend," came the deliberate, perturbed response from behind.

"Yeah, it's my boyfriend," she said triumphantly.

"What the fuck do you think you're doing?" interrogated the voice.

Steven thought he had better face his accuser before his accuser became his offender.

"I was just having a nice conversation with her, that's all. No harm done," Steven stood and stared directly at the man's chin.

"He's an asshole, Jimmy," prodded the women.

"No, Jimmy," explained Steven, "You don't understand. I didn't see a ring. I was just curious, you know."

"He's an asshole, Jimmy," she repeated.

"It's just a friendly misunderstanding," said Peter calmly. Jimmy turned around to find Peter staring into his eyes.

"Who the fuck are you?" Jimmy loudly demanded.

"I'm the asshole's friend," replied Peter.

"Yeah, well then, you're both assholes." Jimmy's arm came up and slapped hard against Peter's chest. Peter swayed but did not step back. Jimmy's eyes grow slightly wider.

Steven's body tensed, and he waited for a signal from Peter.

"I'll take that as the first punch," Peter noted emotionlessly. "Now, you can go into work tomorrow and tell everyone how you got into a fight with two assholes over your girlfriend and how we chickened out, or you can go into work tomorrow and explain how your face got that way."

Peter glared at Jimmy. Jimmy's eyes broke contact, and he looked down at his girlfriend, then back at Peter. Slowly, his hand felt for the back of the chair Steven had occupied and lowered himself into it.

Peter's demeanor changed instantly. He assuredly waved off the approaching waiter, who had become curious about the commotion.

He leaned over the table and sincerely stated, "Jimmy, we're sorry your evening had to start this way. We honestly didn't know she was waiting for you. Can we buy you a drink?"

"Keep your money," came his response. Jimmy took his girlfriend's hand and ignored their presence.

Peter and Steven went back to their table. Steven finished his beer in one extended motion, then motioned for the waiter to bring two more. He moved his chair to cancel any view of the other tables as he attempted to drink from his empty bottle. His head lowered, and he inspected the tablecloth and rearranged his utensils. After several moments of silence, his activity was interrupted by a ball of bread striking him in the forehead from across the table.

He sheepishly peered up at Peter, who was looking at him with his eyebrows raised. Peter's lips were tightly closed together to stifle his laughter.

The absurdity of the events hit Steven at once, and his lips shut too late as his laughter escaped, causing the force of air to create a razzing sound and spittle to fly across the table. His head dipped wildly as his hand slapped against his mouth.

The two men ordered, ate, and imbibed, sharing a few more impromptu laughs.

They left the restaurant full and happy.

It wasn't until they had walked a couple of blocks that they both realized they were underdressed for the cool air that swept off the Pacific. Steven rubbed his forearms as they walked. To take his mind off his chill, he began talking.

"Man, I thought Jimmy was gonna shit himself when he hit you in the chest, and you didn't move," Steven blurted. He hoped Peter would take his cue to add something. Not wanting to lose momentum, he added, "Sometimes I even forget how big you really are."

"Yeah," Peter scoffed. "Jimmy wasn't exactly tiny. It took me about ten seconds to catch my breath. My ribs still hurt."

Steven began to chuckle again. "Yeah, I think Jimmy would have hung me over that deck by my ankles."

"More likely by your balls," clarified Peter.

"I'd have to agree."

They continued to walk, and Steven rethought the entire incident in his head. It was suddenly clear to him the trouble he had been in. He also realized that, if not for Peter, he would be in a lot of pain. His smile faded, and an emotional frown took its place as the two men trudged on against the swirling wind. All at once, he felt the urge to confide his appreciation for Peter's friendship. He acknowledged the beer probably contributed to his sudden emotional state in the same way it contributed to his shoulder occasionally being used to steady himself against the wall of the buildings they passed. He decided if he was going to say it, he needed to do it before the moment was lost.

With his head facing straight ahead, Steven began, "Piper, it just hit me, man. Jimmy was gonna kill me, and there wouldn't have been anything I could have done to stop him. Nice ass would have just sat there and cheered him on." He paused momentarily as he placed his hand on the rim of the sidewalk trash can and negotiated his way around so the two could pass without bumping one another.

His friend's adroitness amused Peter as he watched from fifty feet back. He had stopped at the entrance to McP's Irish Pub. No place better to take the chill off was his thinking. He had started to inform Steven, but his friend began spurting out his confession, and Peter never got the chance. He would just wait for him to finish, but the scene became too enjoyable. So, he stood at the entrance and watched him continue.

"But not you...you took up for me. Even after I cut on you twice, you didn't have anything to do with it, but you stood up for me." Steven halted and turned to face Peter and tell him the most important part of his reflection. When he wasn't there, Steven began to swing his head from side to side and spun around twice with his arms out, looking for his companion.

Peter, now forty yards away, slipped into the doorway of the bar and laughed into his sleeve. He tried his best to ignore the alluring wails of the Irish flute behind him and listened for his abandoned friend. It wasn't long before he heard the acknowledgment he sought.

"Dammit, Piper! Where'd you go, you asshole!" Steven's shouts emitted his slight embarrassment and resignation to being the recipient of Peter's revenge.

Peter turned and entered the bar. Once inside, he was impressed with its atmosphere. It didn't try to be anything but itself. Not overly large, yet able to support a loyal following. The floor was a sturdy wood worn in the appropriate places, telling part of the tale of the pub's long and popular history. The well-worn floor flowed into the dark wood of the bar, which was accented with golden foot rails running its length. It raised itself handsomely upward and was crowned with a light gray marble counter. The marble both accentuated and separated the darkness of the bar, and etched wall paneling. The shelves behind the bar displayed loosely assorted distilled spirits, with just two domestic beers and no fruit-polluted liquors. There were two identical stations for drafts commanding attention along the back wall with enormous, ornate taps jutting from the bronze nozzles. The Irish flutes that had pierced the doorway were replaced by an acoustic guitar and lamenting Gaelic balladeer.

Peter followed the worn path to the back of the establishment, shuffling through random groups and taking note of the few pictures scattered about the walls. He settled on a stool just on the other side of the curved marble, allowing himself a view of the door. The bartender was quick to notice the filled space and approached with a purposeful gait. A few feet from the bar, he swung down the damp cloth from his shoulder onto the cold marble and made the spot new for Peter. "What will it be for you on this night?" Questioned the red-cheeked barkeeper. Peter delighted in the brogue.

"Harp."

"A man's helpin'?"

"Aye...and make it two," replied Peter, slipping into an Irish demeanor and losing himself in the environment.

"I won't leave you stranded. I know you have two hands but only one pipe."

"My friend is on his way."

"Aye...that makes sense now."

The pints of beer arrived as Steven's silhouette appeared over the bartender's shoulder. Peter raised his glass to him, and he worked his way back.

"Oh, I was hoping you'd have a beer waiting, just can't get enough of the stuff."

"Sorry buddy, I can't resist an Irish bar. This place is great, isn't it?"

Steven revolved and nodded his head.

"So, what were you saying?" Peter asked as he raised his glass to his mouth.

"You'll never know," replied Steven, sheepishly. He also raised his glass but quickly replaced it. "Aww...," he grimaced. "Don't need any more of that."

"All right, just let me finish, and we'll get outta here."

Steven nodded his head agreeably, then re-examined his surroundings. The place was nice enough. Although after taking a deep breath, he concluded that bars that smelled more of deodorant and cigars than perfume, weren't his type of place.

He followed the line of faces seated at the bar. He mentally kept tab as he went. "Old man, married couple, old women, loner, loser, date, drunk, double date, loser." His interest in his inventory quickly waned as he neared the opposite end of the bar. Suddenly, his breath halted, his body tensed, and he stood motionless for several moments, focusing his gaze. He maintained his concentration while reaching for Peter's arm.

"No hurry, Piper! This place is growing on me."

Peter was in the process of drinking his beer when Steven's hand grabbed his sleeve. He contorted his body backward and held the disturbed glass from his body. He reached for a napkin to wipe the beer from his chin.

"What?" Asked Peter, wiping off his shirt.

Steven motioned with his eyes, then leaned into Peter and said, "I don't know how I missed her on the way in. Look down the bar at the far end. You may have to take a separate cab."

Peter peered at Steven with a mixture of disbelief, amusement, and disgust. In a tone that represented his disinterest, he said, "Give it a rest, man."

"No, man, I'm serious. Just look."

Peter scoffed, then perused the seated clientele and had no problem identifying Steven's target. He knew she would be attractive, and he was right. But he anticipated an attractive woman whose dubious intentions spoke through her clothing, whose formulated hair and plunging neckline would shriek of her talents and whose presence at this particular bar would either be a misstep or a planned lonesome, less expensive, whiskied head start, designed to open up her personality, in preparation for her appearance at another, more befitting club. He had expected a blemish on the environment.

However, what he found was the exact opposite, and that exposed her just as easily.

She effortlessly blended with her surroundings, yet she was radiant. She was positioned where the bar began, directly across from his view. She sat alone under a bar lamp that provided just enough of a beam to illuminate the worn, well-read book that lay open in front of her. Beside the book was a pint of Guineas Stout, three-quarters full, with the thick, dirty brown foam decorating the sides of the glass.

Her head was angled downward, held in place by an index finger positioned softly against her temple. This placement drew back a significant portion of her shoulder-length auburn hair, allowing an uninhibited view of her face. It was obvious her beauty didn't come from a manufacturer, and that is what struck Peter first. He wasn't concerned with the color of her eyes nor the shape of her nose. He wasn't drawn to the fullness of her lips nor the placement of her cheek bones.

She was natural; she was unconcerned, and she was captivating.

Peter turned to Steven, leaned against his elbow, and defiantly stated, "She's not your type."

106

"What type is that?"

"The type that fetches you orange juice the next morning," answered Peter.

Steven looked her way again, then assured his friend, "I'm not worried about the next morning."

Peter grinned. "Look, I've seen you in action earlier tonight. Don't waste your time. Let me just finish my beer, lad, and we'll head back."

Steven persisted, "There's no harm in asking, right? You don't get the order unless you ask for it. I know you haven't been out of sales that long, Piper."

"Yeah, go tell that to Jimmy," he continued, "She'll see right through you."

"Why are you so concerned, anyway?" Steven interjected, taking a sip of his previously discarded beer. He added pointedly, "I mean, it's not like you'd have any interest."

"My lack of interest has nothing to do with you getting shot down in flames. It only protects you against being shown up," responded Peter flatly.

"Is that right? You know, for a guy who doesn't play anymore, you still talk a big game. Too bad you won't back it up," challenged Steven.

Peter smirked and took another gulp. "Tell you what," he continued, replacing his glass, "The first one to walk out of this bar with her gets the better hotel room at our next stop, wherever that might be."

"I'm paying for it anyway, you bum, but alright, you're on. I'll have you sleeping above the bar yet."

Peter motioned to the bartender, and he approached. "Can't be too sure," he told Steven as they waited. When the bartender arrived, he noticed the unfinished drinks and questioned why he was needed by stating, "I can't wrap those up for ye; they'll leak somethin' awful."

"No, just a wee bit of precaution is all I'll be seekin'," assured Peter again, using his best Irish accent. He switched back while asking, "You see the women at the end of the bar? Do you know if she's alone?"

The bartender did not turn to look. He didn't need to. "How would I know, you suppose? I'm only an immigrant barkeep."

Steven produced a twenty-dollar bill and handed it to the man, who promptly pushed it into his pocket.

"A fine prize for one of ye. Three nights now, she's come in. All three times, she orders a single Guinness and reads a single chapter..." He leaned in, causing Peter and Steven to do the same.

"...alone."

"You can have honors," said Peter, gesturing for Steven to go first.

As Steven confidently rose from his chair, Peter motioned for the bartender to stay a moment longer. They both watched Steven take two steps toward her, then stop and retreat into the men's room as Peter plucked a stack of napkins from the container near him.

When he appeared again, Steven shot his friend a confident glance as he walked purposefully down the bar. He could see the bartender approach her as he walked and hoped he wasn't going to fill her in. Instead, he innocently tapped the bar in front of her as she looked up with a smile and lent him her attention. He did not say anything; he simply placed a stack of cocktail napkins in front of her and gave them a pat. He turned to answer a customer's call, and Steven became grateful he was the one to interrupt her reading. She peeled the top napkin from the stack and brought it toward her face to read the writing. It read:

1.) *Without letting him know, read one napkin every 30*

seconds or so.

2.) *Here he comes.*

Mildly alarmed, she looked up quickly from the paper and tried to discover who had sent her the note. As she examined the patrons, she caught Steven's figure coming toward her and girded herself for their meeting.

"Hi," Steven began with a smile. "It looks like you're enjoying your book, so I won't stay, but you looked so enthralled, I had to come see what you were reading."

She was relieved to know it was a pickup attempt. She couldn't help but smile a little as she evaluated his question. She relaxed her body and decided to play along because she wanted to know what was on the napkins. "It's titled 12 Irish Stories." As she answered, her hand reached for a napkin and read it as she wiped the cover of the book.

He'll start by asking you about the book.

She displayed a whimsical grin as she handed the book to Steven. He accepted it and commented, "This is a fitting place to read it."

"It adds to the flavor," she explained.

"I'm sure it does." He flipped through the pages. "How many have you read so far?"

"Oh, I'm only on my third one." She reached for another napkin and read it before wiping off her beer glass.

He'll ask you your name, then tell you he knows someone with the same one. He'll ask you to spell it.

"It certainly looks interesting...thanks for being so nice." He offered her the book and turned as if to leave. She accepted it and placed it back on the bar, mildly disappointed. Her interest was almost immediately restored when he turned again. "By the way, my name is Steven Cross. It was a pleasure to meet you...?"

Steven extended his hand and mentally congratulated himself when she took his hand and seemed genuinely excited to tell him, "I'm Sarah Garrity."

"Garrity...I should have known it would be Irish." He raised his eyes and repeatedly snapped his fingers, deep in thought, while repeating her name.

"Garrity...Garrity...Garrity...Hey! I used to know a guy named John Garrity from Boston. How do you spell that?"

"G-a-r-r-i-t-y."

"Yep, that's the same way. Do you know him?"

She politely shook her head, then reached for another napkin and read it before wiping the ring of water from the bar.

He'll order a shot of whiskey, then cough for effect as it goes down.

"Where are you from, Sarah?" He asked, sitting on the stool next to her.

She closed her book and concentrated on him. He had trouble hiding his pleasure.

"Well, I grew up in Virginia, but I live in Phoenix now."

"Virginia to Phoenix...wow...Did you move when you got married?"

"No, I'm single...I went to college in San Diego and went back to Virginia for a while after my mom died."

"How long ago did your mom pass?"

"Oh, it's got to be seven years now."

"And how long have you lived in Phoenix?"

"Four."

Steven raised his hand for the bartender. He pointed to Sarah's beer and asked, "Would you like something?" When she declined, he ordered a shot of Jameson. While he watched the bartender tip the bottle, she read another napkin.

He'll insult you in a fun way...your hair, your shoes.

Steven settled with the bartender, held the shot glass on the bar, and asked, "So, what brings you back to San Diego?"

"Oh, my dad lives here. Now, I usually come back once or twice a year and spend a week or so with him. I'm going back in a couple of days."

Steven nodded his head as she spoke. When she was finished, he immediately asked, "So what do you do in Phoenix?"

"Personally or professionally?" She queried.

"Both," he answered, raising the shot glass to his lips.

"Well, personally, I spend a lot of time admiring and exploring the terrain. I studied Geology in College. Professionally, I work..." She lost her train of thought as Steven let out a small cough and winced slightly as he swallowed. Her front teeth clasped her bottom lip as she desperately tried to smother her laughter.

"Excuse me," wheezed Steven, slapping his chest. "Wrong pipe! What were you saying?"

"Oh, nothing really...I was just telling you how I work at the Marriott Resort at Eagles Nest back in Phoenix."

"Well, that's interesting. Yeah." Steven stood back and

examined her outfit. She wore all black. From her onyx earrings to her button-down shirt, to her black jeans, to her silver-toed black boots, she wore black. And even though he knew she looked good in black, he leaned forward, felt the fabric of her shirt, and commented, "I probably would have guessed either an undertaker or a singer with a Johnny Cash cover band." He snickered and squeezed her arm gently so she would know he was kidding. Still quietly laughing while placing his other hand on her knee, he added, "I'm only kidding; don't get mad. I think you look great, really."

She took the opportunity to let go of the laughter she had desperately hidden. She rocked back on her stool, heartily amused. Perhaps, too amused, Steven thought. Nevertheless, he was on a roll.

After several seconds of merriment, Sarah reached for the last napkin, and before wiping away her tears, she read:

1.) The bartender has my license. If you've enjoyed the show,

please play along for two minutes more.

2.) Here I come.

Her first reaction was to search for the bartender. He was already watching and raised the laminated card for her to see. The second thing she did was search for the stranger who had announced

114

his approach. She nodded delicately in response to his index finger over his lips.

"Or maybe a minister's daughter, but it would have to be a sin for me to be thinking the way I am about a minister's daughter, you know. Boy, you sure have the black thing going. I can't stop looking at you," Steven leaned in and moved his hand a few inches up her leg. "You know, Sarah, I'm only in town for a couple more days myself. Maybe we can grab a late dinner, or you could show me the parts of San Diego that only the locals know about? What do you say?"

After Steven finished his close, he found it peculiar that she was staring over his shoulder. He straightened and curiously swiveled to find Peter merging into their space and declared to Steven, in a matter-of-fact tone, "Your time is up."

Peter extended his hand past Steven and directed Sarah, "C'mon, I want to show you the extra pillows at my hotel."

Sarah placed her hand in Peter's and cooed softly as she passed Steven. She pressed her book into his chest and said, "Here you go, Stevie. I won't be needing this tonight."

Steven instinctively clutched the book and stood silently as Peter and Sarah exited the bar.

Before the door could close behind them, Peter was already

pushing it open again. He and Sarah entered the bar and rejoined Steven, who had not moved and still clutched her book against his chest.

Sarah caressed his cheek as she pried the book from his hands, and Peter simply said, "Whose the one with the room above the bar now?"

"Well, fellas, that certainly was an experience. I don't know who you two are, but something tells me you'd be fun to hang out with. Unfortunately, I'm not that daring or nuts, but I really got a kick out of it." Sarah reached into her pockets, feeling around for money.

"No, no..." protested Peter. "I'll pay for your tab. Thanks again! You were a real sport to put up with us like that."

"What do you mean, put up with *us*? What the hell happened?" Demanded Steven.

Peter and Sarah looked at each other and smiled. She waved at the bartender and slipped past them and exited the bar once again.

"What is so funny? Piper, what did you do? You cheated, man. I had her; I was going in for the kill."

"How could I cheat when there weren't any rules?" Consoled Peter as he placed his arm around Steven's shoulder. "Now, bow to the master."

116

"Fuck you."

Steven laughed, still watching the door, "Let's get out of here. We've got a long drive ahead of us tomorrow."

Steven started toward the door, as Peter accepted his license from the bartender and handed him more than enough money to cover the tab and provide a nice tip, then followed.

"Drive?" Questioned Peter. "Where to?"

"Phoenix."

CHAPTER 9

"That's right, Jack. Phoenix."

Peter held the phone under his chin while he rummaged through his pockets, looking for cash. He produced a wad of bills and peeled off a five for the bellman, then whispered he would meet him in the lobby.

"No, I don't know yet. He hasn't told me. All I know is we're leaving in about a half hour and driving over. I figure including a couple of stops, we'll be there within three days. I'll call you from where I'm staying." He shifted the phone to his other ear and reached for the bagel on his nightstand. After taking a larger-than-normal bite, he continued, "How's Tony doing with the camp?"

He listened to Jack Jones' answer while drinking his juice. "Good. All right, Jack. I'll call you when I get to Phoenix. Tell Tony good job, and I'll call him from the road. Take it easy." He ended the call and hastily inspected the room for anything that might have been missed while packing.

Satisfied he had everything, Peter went to the window and faced in the direction of Balboa Park. He tapped the glass with his knuckle, patted his pockets to take inventory of his phone, cash, and wallet, then abruptly turned and headed for the elevator.

In the lobby, Steven was casually going over the bill when he saw Peter exit the elevator. He motioned for him to come over. When he got there, three other clerks gathered.

"They said they have something for us," Steven said, shrugging his shoulders.

"We certainly do," agreed one of the clerks as she coyly presented the two men with a bag. "It's provided everyone here with a lot of laughs."

Steven opened the bag and pulled out a small box. Both men looked at it, trying to imagine what it would contain. They looked blankly at the clerk, and it was then that Peter recognized her as the young lady on duty during his waltz through the lobby in his underwear.

"Underwear, right?" asked Peter, pointing to the tape.

"Yes, sir," she responded proudly as the other clerks chuckled behind her.

"This is the only copy, right?" Peter kidded.

"Oh, no sir..." she happily explained, "...Security demands we keep a copy for our files."

"Well! It will make me feel good to be remembered," relented Peter.

Peter followed Steven through the hotel lobby and exited the building to see the bellman load his bag into the restricted trunk of the white Porsche convertible parked in front.

"I suppose this is another reason why I packed light," he remarked from the top step.

"We might as well have some fun on the way there." Steven passed behind the car and slipped the bellman a tip. He sat in the driver's seat and put on a brown suede cowboy hat and drew the string up to his neck. He reached onto the passenger seat and flipped Peter's hat to him as he approached. "It's rented, anyway. We'll turn it in when we're done. Remember, I'm doing this in Sumner's memory."

Peter examined his hat as they pulled from the driveway and accelerated through the yellow traffic signal on Harbor Drive. "How much cash do you plan on dumping on this trip?" he asked, amused.

Steven's response came in the form of pushing "play" and screaming "Sumner! Sumner! Sumner!" over and over, then maniacally laughing as the music from his playlist blared from the speakers.

****

"Piper?"

Peter opened his eyes to see the inside of his cowboy hat. He had placed it over his face to shade the sun. Slowly, he lifted his arm and cocked the brim so he could get a glimpse of Steven. Steven stared forward, seemingly oblivious to Peter's gaze. The wind was swirling his hair, and his fingers tapped the beat of the music on the steering wheel. Peter lowered the brim and stared up at the ringlets, which allowed small specs of daylight to protrude.

"Peter?"

He knew he heard it that time.

"Yeah?" he answered into his hat.

Several seconds of silence passed until Peter removed his hat and brought his reclined seat back into a straight position. He again turned to Steven, who was still fixated on the miles of road stretching out to the horizon.

"Are you fucking with me?" He prodded.

Steven let the question pass and instead worked on the nerve to ask what was on his mind. Finally, without shifting his vision, in a hesitant and revealing tone, he spoke, "Are you happy?"

Once the question came, Peter did not shift his vision either. Several thoughts entered his mind, and he struggled to grab hold of the answer.

Callous....sarcastic...dismissive...foolish...juvenile. However, a quick review of the circumstances provided him with the conclusion that the question required at least a discriminating response.

"As happy as I should be, I suppose."

"Are you as happy as you were ten years ago?"

"We were different then."

"Different as in happier?"

"Different as in naive."

"Different as in uncompromised?"

"Different as in unscathed."

Both men faced forward and watched the country go by. Although the wind from their speed flowed over them, they could feel the heat it contained, as the green valleys turned into brown desert. Mountains still rose in the background, but the foreground surrendered its color, creating a pale landscape that remained dramatic, nonetheless.

"I don't know," Steven started again, "I should be happier. I know I was once. I always told myself I wouldn't lose who I was, you know? I'd always keep the same ideals and screw everything and anybody that tried to take it away. But somewhere along the line, I forgot what I was supposed to be holding so dear. I woke up one day and realized I was empty. I was gray, you know? Everything that had given me purpose was drained, and I didn't even notice it going. How can that happen?"

He paused, but both of them knew he had more to say. Peter waited.

"That's why I came back...That's why I waited for you in the gym that night."

"And what did you find out?" probed Peter.

"That you held on to it...whatever it is."

This time, the silence was labored as both searched for clarification.

"Pull over."

"What?"

"Pull over. I want to show you something."

Steven eased the car to a stop and curiously watched as Peter opened his door and walked several feet into the brown environment.

"Come here for a minute," Peter waved Steven toward him.

Steven pulled the emergency brake and, with a deliberate sigh, exited the car and entered the terrain with his palms up, asking for a reason.

"Turn around," said Peter, twirling his hand above his head.

Steven turned himself quickly and impatiently questioned, "Ok, so what?"

"So, what do you see?"

"Not much."

"C'mon, try harder."

"I see brown splotches of dried-out grass...spindly trees that look half-dead. I see a couple of cactus over there...and some twigs."

"Ok, that's better," Peter encouraged. "Stay with me. How 'bout the car?"

"Yeah, I see the car. That's obvious."

"Depends on who's looking. If I asked the same question to a stranger, he may well list the car first. It looks astonishing against the landscape." Peter turned around and then continued, "You saw some twigs; I see a packrat's nest. You saw a couple of cactus; I see three different types of cacti. You saw half-dead trees; I see a Mesquite tree. You saw dried grass; I see camouflage. We're in rattlesnake country now. You see empty; I see an ecosystem."

The mere mention of rattlesnakes caused Steven to search the terrain with determination. Peter stepped forward and turned him by the shoulders, saying, "I see miles of depraved and thirsty creation laying the foundation for snow-capped mountains. I see snow-capped mountains outlined by the bluest of skies, and the bluest of skies dotted by puffs of white clouds..." Peter knelt and gathered a handful of dirt, letting it run through his hands as he finished. "...And I see a piece of earth that may never have been touched by another human hand before."

Steven stood still and waited for an explanation.

Peter inhaled deeply and summarized, "We're both in the same place, yet we experience it differently...not necessarily better, just differently. The point is you have the same choice no matter where you are or what you're doing. You can choose to view a situation or environment any way you want and the "it" you say you've lost. I'm just trying to let you know you still have it; you just shut it off. You can look at a flower and think about pollen and allergies if you choose, but chances are you'll get more pleasure from it if you see its beauty."

They turned together and walked back to the road where the car waited. As they neared, Steven handed the keys to Peter.

"Here, you drive. I want to experience my surroundings."

They climbed into the car, and as Peter drove off, Steven put his hat over his face and reclined his seat.

CHAPTER 10

"**W**ould you know if Sarah Garrity is an employee here?" Steven leaned over the check-in desk at the Marriott at Eagles Nest and whispered to the clerk. He did not want Peter to know why he had chosen Phoenix just yet and had to wait until he walked several feet away to investigate Sarah's whereabouts.

The clerk finished typing the current line of information and inspected Steven. "Yes, sir. Ms. Garrity just returned this morning."

Steven leaned further forward on his elbows, "Good. Could you tell me where I might find her?"

The clerk could not detect any animosity in her questioner's voice but asked anyway, "Is there something I can help with, sir?"

Steven anxiously checked Peter's position, then responded, "No, no. I'm just an old friend, and I remember her telling me she worked here. I thought I would surprise her." His toes were now the only part of his shoes that touched the floor.

"I see," she whispered. "I'm not sure where she is at the moment, Mr. Cross, but I can certainly call."

Steven waived his arms. "No, that's alright. Don't get her in any trouble."

The clerk inspected him again and assured him, "I don't think it's a concern. Ms. Garrity is the General Manager of the resort."

Steven pushed off the counter as if it had emitted an electric shock and stood straight. His right hand came up and scratched the back of his head, and he felt the gritty remains of the desert wind. The clerk continued to watch as he mouthed the word "Wow" and then bobbed his head and mouthed the word "Cool."

He glanced at his watch and realized it was after 6:00. He stepped to the counter once again and inquired, "What time does Ms. Garrity usually leave for the day?"

"It usually depends on the day's scheduled functions, but on Sundays, usually not past 7:00."

"I see," acknowledged Steven. "Are there activities planned this week?"

The clerk opened the drawer beneath the counter and took out the weekly schedule of guest events. She perused it for a few seconds, then responded, "Well, tomorrow at 6:00 p.m., there is the cocktail reception for all guests of the hotel, then Thursday-"

"Will she attend tomorrow evening?" Steven politely interrupted.

"Why, yes, sir, she makes it a point to be there."

"Very well. I'll catch up with her tomorrow, but I'd still prefer to surprise her if you wouldn't mind not telling her I asked for her," Steven pleasantly requested.

"I understand," The clerk smiled and handed him two sets of room keys. "Mr. Max is staying on our executive level, which is located on the top two floors of the resort." She paused and inspected Steven for a third time. She pointed to his envelope and stated, "Mr. Cross, you will be staying in our deluxe accommodations located down the hall past the health club and up one flight." Before she let go of his envelope, she added, "Is that correct?"

Catching her meaning, he smirked, shrugged his shoulders, and simply explained, "Lost a bet."

Steven thanked her and turned to find Peter leafing through the tourist information pamphlets. Loudly, he announced, "Piper, I put you as far away from me as possible. There's a special access key to get you onto your floor. You want to see the broom closet I'm in, asshole?"

"No need. I'm sure it would be too crowded for both of us. I'm beat anyway. I'm just going to stretch out in my Jacuzzi and read up on the great city of Phoenix. You did get me a Jacuzzi, right?"

Steven deflected the sarcastic question to the front desk clerk, who nodded her head.

"Of course," confirmed Steven. "I'll catch up with you in the morning. You plan the day tomorrow. I just want to be back for the cocktail reception. I heard it's fantastic."

CHAPTER 11

It was 6:25 p.m. when Steven walked alone into the partitioned ballroom where the cocktail reception was being held. The two friends ended their round of golf just after 2:00 p.m., and Peter requested to borrow the car and head into Phoenix.

As he entered slowly, Steven was pleased to realize his assumptions about the gathering were correct. He had hoped for a total of about forty people, and he was right. He had imagined the average age at about fifty, but it was more like sixty. The only thing that brought the average down was the handful of twenty-something children of guests attracted to the allure of free drinks and food. Steven passed just such a group as he made his way to the bar, being sure to go behind the most attractive of the bunch, placing his right hand on her shoulder, whispering pleasantly in her ear, "Excuse me, please," while his left hand ever so slightly felt the outline of her ass. Innocent enough, he thought to himself, while ordering a vodka tonic from the white-jacketed retiree behind the portable bar.

Steven let his eyes pass the separate small groups of random guests that dotted the room as his drink was being made. Almost immediately, he spotted Sarah chatting dutifully with a well-seasoned couple. He moved closer and heard them telling her about their Minneapolis trip to find out if the heat would be too much for them to take if they decided to buy a winter home in town. She listened intently, then asked if they had decided.

"Well, she's always cold anyway, so she would move in a minute." started the gentleman, "But I'd sure miss the ice fishing." The man's wife added, "Oh yes, God help him if he can't spend eight hours sitting on a frozen lake, in some broken down hut the size of an outhouse, eating greasy food and getting drunk with his buddies. Do you know how many fish he brought home last year? Four. And guess who got to clean and cook them." The woman pointed to herself as she cocked an eyebrow.

Sarah smiled and interjected, "Well then, we'll have to get you to move to Phoenix so he can take up golf." She turned to the gentleman, gently squeezed his forearm, and winked. He smiled back appreciatively. She continued, "I hope you enjoy the rest of your stay at the resort. Please let me know if we can provide any type of assistance while you are here. It was a pleasure meeting you, Mr. & Mrs. Wallace."

As Sarah turned to make her way to another group, she found herself standing directly in front of Steven Cross. She stopped abruptly, swayed backward, and gazed at him. Immediately noticing he was by himself, her first thought was, "Businessman." She followed that thought with, "Pretty cute businessman." She ended her thoughts there and began the conversation. "Good evening, sir. I'm..."

"You must be on the seventh story by now," Steven interrupted.

Sarah's mind raced to find some meaning in what he said. "Excuse me?" she asked.

"Your Irish short stories...one a day, right?"

Her mind raced again, trying to place the context of what he said. Suddenly, she acknowledged his opening by dropping her head to her chest while shaking it slowly from side to side. She looked up and replied, "I apologize. I didn't recognize you without your partner in crime. Will he be by shortly to escort me away again?"

"Oh, him. No, it's just me."

"Ok, just you. So, what's tonight's game?"

"No games. I was just wondering if you knew where I could find a good Irish bar?"

"San Diego," she replied matter of factly. She looked past Steven to set her course. "Now, it was a surprise to see you again, but I have to..."

"Wait," Steven said, dipping his upper body in her chosen path. "Aren't you just a little flattered I would drive all the way to Phoenix to see you again?"

Maintaining her friendly approach but emphasizing her control of the situation, she coolly replied, "Actually, I'm a little scared that you would follow me here."

"Well, that's not the answer I hoped for. Although now that you mention it, I don't blame you for feeling that way," Steven acknowledged. "Let me take a moment to explain that Peter and I are on a trip without schedules. We choose where to go next by things that happen along the way. Gut feeling, so to speak. If we didn't come here, we'd probably still be in San Diego waiting for a sign."

"So, I gave you a sign?" questioned Sarah with authority.

"As good as any."

"And what might that sign have been?"

Steven's mind raced now. He crossed his arms and nervously smiled at Sarah, who didn't change her expression.

"This is an important response, isn't it? I could further your fear of me or just plain piss you off if I'm not careful with this one."

"How 'bout the real reason?" pushed Sarah.

"How 'bout that I wanted to come to Phoenix and talk with

you because our conversation the other night was based on a stupid but well-meaning bet, and I needed to know if you were at all interested in getting to know me...even if that means my feelings might get a little bruised in the process." Steven unfolded his arms and let them drop to his sides. He let his eyes wander from Sarah's and looked down for a moment, then back at her.

"Prepare for a black and blue ego," quipped Sarah.

"Aww, you can't mean that Sarah...see, I even remembered your name."

"I'm wearing a name badge."

"Oh...I didn't notice, I swear. C'mon, I'll make you a deal. I'll be staying in your hotel for the next several days and spending lots of cash. All I want from you is a fair shot. I'm an acquired taste. And I'm harmless. A little conversation here and there won't hurt. You never know. You might change your mind about me."

Sarah crossed her arms and simply replied, "You are a welcome guest at the resort, and if you need assistance with anything, please let us know. Now, if you'll excuse me, it's time for me to check in with the chef at our restaurant."

"I understand. Chefs are notoriously tense individuals. Better not keep him waiting." Steven stepped aside and motioned with his arm for Sarah to pass. He refrained from allowing his free hand to brush against her ass as she went by, although he watched as she moved away.

After a few steps, she glanced over her shoulder. "Two things. First, the chef's a woman. Second, nice touch wearing black, but it really doesn't work for you." She focused her head forward again and left the reception.

Smart girl, thought Steven, as he glanced down at his newly purchased outfit.

CHAPTER 12

The Eagle's Nest Marriott pool area made the most of its design. When the resort was built, the pool was obviously considered a necessity but nothing more. However, its lack of imagination was smothered over the years by impeccable landscaping. Large, healthy hibiscus plants lined the walkways, and the grass was full, vibrant, and weedless.

As Peter walked the perimeter of the pool, he examined the surroundings. He appreciated the work of the grounds crew, but he was more interested in the people decorating or, more importantly, spoiling the environment. His eyes fixated on them as he passed while searching for the spot where he would spend his day.

"Cougher... loud talker... splasher... fidgeter... complainer... ahh... reader." Peter spread his long towel over the lounge chair next to a middle-aged woman reading a rather thick paperback. He spied the title as he prepared his space. It read "Medieval Desires" and had a guy on the front who looked a lot like a surfer. Ok, so it wasn't War and Peace, but at least it would keep her busy.

Peter had just become comfortable in his lounge chair. He had found the spot where the rods and plastic straps align perfectly with the appropriate body parts. Content, he exhaled deeply and welcomed his comfortable status.

"Good late morning, sir." Peter exhaled deeply again and peered at a shapely form silhouetted by the sun. "I was told to give you these and wait." The poolside waitress handed Peter three folded cocktail napkins. The first one read:

Order a Banana Daiquiri

After reading the napkin, Peter glanced at the waitress and asked, "Do I have to?" She gestured toward the second napkin. Peter opened it, and it read:

Yes, you have to

"You're not going to make me say it, are you?"

Before the waitress could respond, Peter read the third napkin.

You have to say it

"Can I get a banana daiquiri, please?"

Peter wondered how Steven had learned of his napkin messages in San Diego. He had never mentioned it since it may have come in handy again during this trip. Although he was found out, the banana daiquiri would taste sweet. He would toast his friend whenever he arrived and tell him that ordering a feminine drink from a scantily clad waitress was a small price to pay for winning their bet.

The tray with his drink returned a few minutes later, but this time, as he peered into the sun, he viewed the silhouette of a woman wearing a sundress. The light from behind allowed for a startling glimpse of the shape of the legs under the garment.

"I thought I'd pour water on the next round of your games while it was still early."

Peter sat up straight and cupped his hands over his eyes. He recognized her right away.

"It's nice to see you again," he said. "But I have no idea what you're talking about."

Sarah handed him the daiquiri and sat on the edge of the lounge chair beside him. "I already spoke with your partner last night at the guest reception. I clarified for him that what was once fun would be annoying if done twice."

"Especially if everyone isn't playing," deadpanned Peter.

"So, you aren't part of this?" queried Sarah.

"Again, I don't know what you're talking about, but I'm trying not to be part of anything on this trip, much less twice."

"So, you drove from San Diego to Phoenix without knowing

why?"

"The 'why' is up for grabs on this trip. It's more about 'why not?' Steven's looking for the meaning of life, and I'm his sidekick. Not a bad deal, considering he might share it with me if he finds it."

"No schedule?"

"Do we act like we're on a schedule?"

"No, in fact, you act like you don't have a care in the world."

Peter paused, then retorted, "Yeah, that might be the shame of it all, huh?"

Sarah stood and thought for a moment. "I'm sorry if my assumptions were off base. It seems I may need to give a little more credence to your friend's side of why the two of you are here."

"And what did my friend say about why we were here?" asked Peter.

"It doesn't really matter. I'm glad to know it wasn't round two of a game with me as the prize."

"Oh, it may well be round two for Steven. But rest assured, I'm out."

"I'll keep my wits about me then," said Sarah playfully. She stood to leave.

"It was nice seeing you again, Sarah," offered Peter.

Sarah smiled, then squinted as if she realized a flaw in the conversation. "Did I ever tell you my name?" she questioned, knowing the answer was no.

"You're wearing a name tag," replied Peter as he eased his way back into his lounge chair. "Sweet job. I hope my drink is on you."

CHAPTER 13

I t was 5:30 p.m. when Peter exited the shower, dried off, and cinched the towel tightly around his waist. He picked up the phone and dialed Steven's room again. When no one answered, he dialed the front desk.

"Good evening, Mr. Max. How can I help you?"

"Good evening," answered Peter. "I've been dialing Steven Cross' room several times but haven't gotten an answer. I wanted to be sure I have the right number."

"Just one moment, sir, and I'll try and connect you."

Peter heard the line ring twice, and then Steven answered.

"Hello."

"Hey. Did you just get in?"

"No. I've been back for a couple of hours or so."

"I've been trying to call. What's your room number again?"

Peter waited for an answer. Finally, Steven admitted, "1218."

"No wonder I wasn't getting an answer at 102, Jackass. When did you change rooms?" challenged Peter.

"Last night. We never said I had to stay in that dump more than one night. I paid off my bet," defended Steven.

"Fair enough. Let's make another bet for the dinner tab tonight."

"I think I'm being set up, but ok, what's the bet?"

"I'll bet you I know why you chose to come to Phoenix and stay at this hotel."

Steven let out a small guilty chuckle. "When did you see her?"

"She saw me at the pool this morning. Seems she thought I was part of your grand scheme."

"You didn't ruin my chances, did you?" Steven asked quickly.

"I didn't realize you had chances to ruin when it came to her," replied Peter.

"We'll see. She definitely has me thinking, though. Something about her draws me in. I can't quite put my finger on it."

"Maybe it's because she's respectable. You haven't encountered that in a while."

"Maybe," confessed Steven. "I forgot how much I like that."

Through the phone line, Peter heard a giggly voice in the

background: "I know something else you like." Suddenly, the phone went silent, and Peter knew Steven had abruptly cupped his hand over the phone receiver. After a couple of seconds, Steven spoke, "You win, Piper. Dinner's on me. How 'bout we meet in the bar at 7:00? We'll see what kind of food the Eagle's Nest serves."

"Look, if you want to have dinner with your roommate, that's OK. I'll make do," offered Peter.

"No, no," denied Steven. "You know me. By 7:00, that will be a distant memory."

"Yeah. I'm beginning to know that all too well. I'll see you at 7:00."

Peter hung up the phone and sat heavily on the bed. For the first time in a long time, he questioned if he didn't know what the hell was going on in the world. It wasn't Steven fucking everyone that irritated him; it was everyone who was fucking Steven. It just seemed like that was the way most people kept score of their lives anymore. Sex. Meaningless, faceless, nameless, unemotional, complication-free, sometimes sweatless, enjoyable fucking. It used to be that 'Wham, bam, thank you ma'am' was a term used in guys' locker rooms. These days, Peter got the impression a women's reply to that statement would be a hearty, "You're welcome...it was a pleasure having your cock in me. What was your name again?"

Still, there was a part of him that lamented not being a part of it. And that made him curse it, and himself, even more.

CHAPTER 14

"I'll have another." Peter waived the glass of bourbon-coated ice in front of him, and the bartender nodded affirmatively as he passed with another couple's drinks. The restaurant bar was dimly lit, and usually, Peter would have found a corner bar stool to take advantage of the shadows. But the only TV was toward the front of the bar, and he decided to bring himself up to date on what was happening in the world of sports. The bartender returned with a generous pour and placed it in front of Peter. "Thanks, Tony," said Peter.

"Of course," came Tony's reply. "Can I get you anything else?"

Peter started to wave him off, then asked, "Hey, I've been out of the loop for a couple of weeks. Have I missed anything?"

"Let's see," thought Tony. "The Diamondbacks are still three games back, the Suns don't know what they're doing, and the Cardinals. Ohhh, man, don't even get me started."

"In other words, same old shit," stated Peter.

"Pretty much sums it up," replied Tony as he washed and rinsed glasses.

Peter considered asking him if he knew of anything that might have happened outside of Arizona when he heard a familiar voice from behind.

"Hi, Tony," she started. "I just spoke with Bill about the two large groups we have dining with us tonight. He's a little concerned there might be a slight wait, fifteen minutes or so, if they both come at once. Are you ok to handle a little overflow in about an hour?"

"Yes, ma'am," answered Tony. "I'll be sure to make it a pleasant part of their evening."

"Thanks. Never doubted that."

"Every detail covered, Miss Garrity. Somehow, I would have never doubted that about you either." Peter turned to face Sarah as he spoke, and she reacted as if pleasantly surprised.

"We have to stop meeting in bars, Mr. Max!" she playfully responded.

"I'm not wearing a name badge, so how did you know my name?" inquired Peter.

"Every detail, Mr. Max. You said it yourself."

"My compliments. First name, please."

"If you prefer."

"No, I'm asking if you know my first name?" he quizzed.

Sarah tilted her head slightly and shot him a pseudo-annoyed look. "Peter. Not Pete. Peter."

Peter couldn't help but smile. "I'm impressed. And put in my place. Now, please call me Peter. You can forget my last name if you want."

"Done. Please do me the same favor."

"Very well. Sarah and Peter, it is."

They shook hands and smiled once again.

THOMAS K. SHANNON

CHAPTER 15

Peter stared at the drawn curtains, watching a single ray of sunlight grow stronger as the day threw off its darkness. Funny, he thought, how the curtains were still blocking 99% of the light, but one ray forced itself through, thereby causing a forfeit of design. Then, he thought, this is how I think after no sleep.

He arose with no purpose and swayed toward the bathroom sink. Once there, he filled his cupped hands with cold water and dove into them on three separate occasions. After dragging a small white towel across his face, he lingered on his reflection and stared. His expression was studious but without emotion. He was taking stock.

The glass told him the truth, and he appreciated that. He knew for a while that his hair was beginning to show a few strands of gray, and his face was becoming more rugged. Rugged…that was a word reserved for guys who didn't want to say they were getting wrinkles. Time treated him no differently than anyone who came before him.

It was shaping, defining, refining, and carving his features as it passed. He didn't mind. In fact, Peter welcomed time. He welcomed its pace. Finally, after a few seconds, he acknowledged, "Well," he spoke to his reflection, "you're still here to remind yourself. I'm proud of ya! Keep reminding yourself, you fucker. Carry it with you. You deserve it."

Peter approached the lobby door and was greeted by a fresh voice full of enthusiasm. "Good morning, sir!" said the concierge as he set a course to get to the door first. "Heading out for a run?"

Peter smiled. "Yes, I am, but not necessarily here. Is there a park nearby?"

"There is a jogging trail that begins just down the hill. Most of our guests…"

"Yes, I know about the trail, thanks. But, I am more interested in a park…you know, swings, sandbox, Frisbees, maybe a few other joggers." And with difficulty, Peter added, "…Mothers and children."

The concierge gave a quizzical look toward Peter. He had followed along until the mother and children remark. Peter understood his look but pressed him by widening his eyes and raising his eyebrows.

"Well, yes, sir, there is. But you will need to take a cab. It's a few exits down I-17. Funny, taking a cab to go for a run." The concierge let out a slight chuckle to reward his own sense of humor. Peter smiled politely.

"That will be fine. Can you call one for me?"

"With pleasure! Right this way!" With one practiced motion, the concierge swung the lobby door open and gestured for Peter to exit first with an exaggerated wave of his other arm. Once outside, Peter could see the cab awaiting its next passenger. The hotel had enough guests who would need rides to the airport that cabs always waited in the carport. Together, they approached the cab, and by design, the concierge reached the vehicle first and, in ballet-like fashion, pivoted, grabbed the door handle, and pulled it open.

Peter entered the cab, continuing the orchestrated event by sliding a $5 bill into the concierge's hand, which not coincidentally was positioned perfectly for such a gratuity.

"Why, thank you, sir! That is quite kind."

"Not at all. You've been helpful...and exceedingly upbeat. Just something to help begin your shift."

"Oh, I've been here all night...I get off in twenty minutes." The concierge closed the door, re-positioned his head next to the front passenger window, and addressed the cab driver. "Adobe Dam Park. The gentlemen would like to go for a nice jog." The cabbie shook his head affirmatively and shifted into drive.

The cabbie was also helpful. After learning Peter wanted a course of about five or six miles, he dropped him at a place in the park that would allow for just that. He also took into account Peter's wish to sit and rest near a playground. The cabbie had assured him he would come across a very popular playground about four miles into his lap around the park.

Sure enough, it was there. And it was crowded. So crowded, Peter kept his distance. He had to...there wasn't a seat near the actual playground. Mothers and even some dads had staked their claims for good vantage points of their children. In this world, a parent could not take any chances. Neither could a concierge, thought Peter. His odd want to see mothers with their children was matched by a place that would not allow a stranger with ill thoughts to carry out any sort of plan. No, these parents were aware and positioned appropriately. "Well done. That was five bucks well spent."

Peter settled in about thirty yards from the playground and watched. The distance was short enough to allow for good vision yet sufficiently far enough away to prohibit two things; attention and company. He searched for a pair that met his initial qualifications…A young mother with a young daughter. A mother who was not too sure of herself when it came to parenting but amazing with her instincts, and a young daughter who was discovering things every day and who trusted her mother completely.

There was to be no father in his scenario. The father was missing. The father was delinquent. The father chose not to come along.

Peter absorbed the happenings at that playground for six hours as others came and went. He never spoke a word and kept his focus the entire time.

THOMAS K. SHANNON

CHAPTER 16

Steven returned from the steam room to see the red light on his phone alerting him to a waiting message. He discarded the damp towel as he casually walked around the bed and sat at its edge. He searched the phone's facade, then pressed the appropriate button for voicemail.

"Steven, it's Pip...Peter. Listen, it's about 5:30, and I'm not up for much conversation or another four-star meal. I'm going to hang out here and watch something stupid on TV. I'll be regrouped by tomorrow. Anyway, I can't imagine I'll be getting a protest call as I've just cleared the path for your end game. After all, no need to let her know before she arrives at the restaurant, right? It's just a casual dinner...platonic even...right? Feel free to make me as sick as you need to convince her of that and keep her at the table. After she stays, well, you'll have to come up with something beyond your usual...believe me. You have an hour and a half...better start thinking. Oh, and you are going to have to control that smile on your face..."

As Steven replaced the receiver, he realized he was smiling and quickly rubbed the back of his hand across his lips, erasing any trace of it. But, as he pushed himself aloft, it returned.

Sarah arrived at Saguaros at 6:40 p.m. As she pulled up the driveway toward the restaurant's entrance, the valet recognized her vehicle and sprang into action, removing an orange cone and inviting the convertible into a space right next to the front door. Perks had become commonplace among the people who orchestrated the hospitality of Greater Phoenix. Her relationship with the General Manager at Saguaros was no different. In fact, before her arrival, she had called him to confirm she was the first of the party of three to arrive. He assured her that while the lounge was somewhat busy, only couples and single men looking for single women occupied its space.

She had asked if two gentlemen had taken up shop, to which the reply was no. Had it been a yes, she would have simply waited in her car until 7:15. Now, she would have the advantage of watching them enter…her turf, after all. She had done an excellent job of keeping control of the situations thus far. Now, when they entered, she would either be seemingly engaged with one of the single men looking for single women or greet them in a business-like demeanor…she would decide within the next few minutes.

Sarah glanced at the rearview mirror out of habit, then exited her car with a genuine smile of gratitude for Oscar, who had so eagerly guided her car as if she had just arrived from the red carpets of Hollywood. "Oscar!" She beamed, "How have you been? You look well."

Oscar smiled brightly as he greeted Sarah, but then his smile turned consciously dour, and he mocked-scolded her with his index finger. "Where have you been? You know I can't stand not seeing you for more than a month at a time…I get the shakes!!"

"Oh, stop it!" She returned, high-fiving him and passing off the keys as she passed. She learned long ago that a tip insulted their relationship. "You know that space is worth an extra $50 every night I'm not here."

"And I'd pass it up 364 more times if it meant seeing you each day. I know that's sappy, but it's the truth."

It had been seven years since she had gone out on a limb and convinced the GM at Saguaros to hire Oscar. He had previously worked at the Eagle's Nest before she was in any position to prevent his dismissal, but she knew of his work ethic. So what if he didn't make an exceptional waiter due to his clumsy hands? His customer service was legendary. It was perhaps the first favor she called in for a friend, but his flawless performance as a valet since arriving at Saguaros began her reputation as the real deal when it came to sizing up talent. And her looking out for a friend with three small children instantly made her infallible to the rest of her staff.

Saguaros overcame its touristy name with décor, service, and menu. In the restaurant business, a great location and a catchy name can start you off fast, but that will only last so long. Décor, service, and a sturdy menu will make customers get in their car to get a fix.

At the entrance to the restaurant stood two fourteen-foot wooden doors ornately carved with southwestern appeal. Once inside, the lighting progressively got slightly brighter but never bright. Subconsciously, one got the sense of being brought forward, entering, being enlightened, and becoming part of the scene. Dark wood, brown and black leather chairs, and the black carpet made the white tablecloths seemingly hover in mid-air and invited the eye to focus on the extraordinary presentation of succulent foods and mouthwatering aromas.

Sarah enjoyed the subtleties of the restaurant as she approached the Maître D'. She was met before reaching her mark by Marc Sweeney, the General Manager. "Ahhh, Sarah! You are the sight as always…" Marc and Sarah embraced as the friends they were, and she smiled appreciatively as she pulled on his elbow and questioned him in a whispered voice, "I'm going for attractive without setting any expectations…what's the verdict?"

Marc stepped back and leaned on his right foot, quickly

examining. In an instant, he reached for the scarf tied around her neck and repositioned the knot from the right side to the left. "That was so I could say I found something wrong. I didn't," he offered.

Sarah shot back a sarcastic but surrendering look and kept the scarf as he left it.

"All right, then," Marc continued. "I have your table ready for you, but as we just confirmed on the phone, no one else from your party has checked in, and all the gentlemen in the lounge are by themselves. Where would you like to go?"

"Lounge," came her one-word reply.

"My pleasure," Marc extended his arm, and Sarah gently took his lead as he escorted her toward the lounge.

Sarah surveyed the room as they turned the corner, searching for the spot where she wanted to sit and greet her guests when they arrived. But she stopped quickly as she spied Steven Cross at the end of the bar, already positioned so he could see who entered the room.

Marc came to a stop when he felt his arm remain at the entrance, and Sarah's hand tighten on his sleeve. He saw her eyes gazing forward and asked, "What's the matter?"

Sarah looked at Marc and simply remarked, "Nothing. My mistake. It was supposed to be two, but alas, I am being greeted by the lone wolf." She moved forward with a convincing gait that disallowed any notion she was caught off guard.

Marc reassured her, "I wonder if the lone wolf knows he is dining with the lioness?"

"Oh, I'm not that mean."

"Indeed not. But just as protective of your territory."

Sarah patted Marc's hand as they walked.

Steven stood as the couple approached his outpost, "Good evening, Sarah. It appears you are in good hands."

Marc instinctively replied, "Good is debatable, sir. Loyal might be a better adjective. Precious soul, this." Marc patted Sarah's arm, still leaving his eyes on Steven.

Steven stared for a moment into Marc's eyes, then smiled widely in acceptance, offered his arm to Sarah, and turned his gaze toward her. "Will you make the exchange from loyal to warned, then?"

Sarah let a small laugh escape as she took Steven's sleeve and sat down. "It appears you two have not met yet. Steven, I would like you to meet a very good friend of mine, Marc Sweeney. Marc, this is Steven Cross."

Marc and Steven extended their hands at the same time and acknowledged each other in a friendly fashion. Steven added,

"…friend in training."

"It is a pleasure to meet you, Mr. Cross. A friend of Sarah's is a friend of this establishment. Please make yourself at home and let me know of anything you need. With that, I'll take my leave and let you continue training." Marc bowed slightly as a professional courtesy, smiled at Sarah, and immediately caught the gaze of the bartender and moved his eyes in such a way that meant there would be no bill in the lounge. The bartender simply nodded once. Marc retreated two steps, pivoted, and exited the lounge.

The last thing he heard was Steven saying, "You look wonderful. I really like your scarf."

Sarah smiled, touched the knot on the left side of her neck, and acknowledged, "Oh, thank you. I had forgotten I'd worn it."

"Oh," Steven started as he settled back into his chair, "somehow, I don't think you do anything without thinking it through first."

"My…that would make me easily read. I hope there is more to me than that."

"I'm convinced there is…I'm betting on it."

"Just don't count on it."

"How long might I get to figure it out?"

"For now, the time it takes to have dinner."

"I've always been good under pressure."

"Oh, don't put pressure on yourself. I'd hate to see you freeze up. That would make for some periods of awkward silence. It being just you and me and all."

"Yes….that. Peter sends his regrets."

"How regrettable."

The bartender picked the brief silence that followed to make himself known, "Hello, Ms. Garrity. It is great to see you back. Shall I bring you a glass of Conundrum?"

Sarah smiled sweetly toward the bartender and said, "I think I'll simply have an iced tea for now, Charles. Thank you."

"Annnnd, thud," announced Steven, as Charles went away.

"Excuse me?" Asked Sarah as if she didn't know what he meant.

Steven raised his rock glass and downed the remaining portion of brown liquid before stating, "Thud…as in boom…as in bam…as in transparent…which leads to BOO and hiss!"

Charles came back with Sarah's iced tea and asked Steven, "Another Blue for you, sir?"

"Why, no, thank you." Steven lamented, "I think I'll switch to iced tea."

Charles took his cue and filled another tall glass with ice, then went to get another iced tea. Sarah squared in her chair. Steven lowered his head a bit and formulated his next remarks. He relaxed into his chair and raised his eyebrows as if to say, "Is this how it's going to be?"

Sarah simply raised her eyebrows in response and tilted her head slightly as if to say, "It looks that way."

Steven opened his mouth and drew in a breath, then started, "Ok, couple of things. First, I received a message from Peter at 5:30 saying he was not interested in leaving his room tonight. He didn't say why, but I could tell he had made up his mind. I'll chalk it up to being with me for over two weeks. After all, we left Baltimore on the 4th and it's what, like the 18th now? That's a long time to put up with this mug, much less this mouth." Steven paused and looked at Sarah. No expression. He continued.

"Sooo, at 5:35, I made the decision not to track you down. I simply would keep our plans. I am still interested in having dinner with you and hopefully enjoying our conversation. I didn't know how awkward this would be, but I knew it could be extremely so. But here is the thing. It's obvious I am on your property. It's also obvious you could be falling down drunk and still possess the ability to leave me. No doubt we will not be interacting beyond an enjoyable conversation. I….get…that."

Steven raised his eyebrows again as if to say, "Do you believe me?"

Sarah raised her eyebrows and tilted her head as if to reply, "Say it out loud."

Steven pressed on, "Alright, that brings us to this…Obviously, Charles is used to you enjoying a glass of white wine. I would venture to say on the rare occasions you are able to leave the Eagle's Nest and take in some free time, you also enjoy a glass of white wine. Me I've been enjoying myself too much lately, but I would still like nothing more than for you to enjoy a glass of wine. I will say this once, and if I cannot convince you of my sincerity, I believe we should both drink our iced teas and call it a night."

Steven leaned forward to finish his statement, and an intrigued Sarah mirrored his movement, "You will not be touching me tonight."

Sarah couldn't help it. She laughed and bounced backward into her chair.

Steven stayed in his position but matched her changed demeanor with a smile. "Deal?"

Charles came back with Steven's iced tea. Sarah asked him simply, "Charles, would you mind bringing me that Conundrum and Mr. Cross his Johnny Walker?"

"Surely, Ms. Garrity."

Steven fell back into his chair, wiped his brow, and took a long sip of the iced tea. With a grimace, he exclaimed, "Ahh, geez! That's awful."

Sarah laughed again. "Unfortunately, Mr. Cross, there is something wrong with what you just told me."

"And what might that be?"

"It's not the 18th. Today is the 20th."

Steve glanced at the date on his watch, then tapped the face with his index finger, "How unfortunate. I hope you believed the rest."

"Oh, it's a certainty."

"June 20th. Time flies, I suppose. June 20th, hmmm. June 20th...." Steven's voice trailed off as he repeated the date. He suddenly knew why Peter did not join them tonight. And for the briefest of moments, he acknowledged the date within his own mind and felt a pang of guilt for minimizing its meaning. But, just as quickly, he assured himself what was done was done. His response to today's date was right in front of him.

THOMAS K. SHANNON

CHAPTER 17

Among Steven Cross' previously determined facts of life was this: timing is as important as skill or luck. Further, timing is a skill that separates good from great, memorable from forgettable, and accomplishments from wishful thinking. For those who would argue his take was just a play on the adage "Timing is everything," he would quickly correct that timing isn't everything; it merely sets up the happenings that might follow if appropriately executed. You'd still have to complete the task at hand. Timing placed sports heroes with the ball just before the buzzer, or business people at the negotiation table at the apex of a deal. But whoever finds themself in that position must still perform.

That is why, upon arriving at their table, Steven immediately decided not to waste the timing he was just given. The extent of Sarah's relationship with the team at Saguaros was cemented as he realized they were being seated at the most exquisite real estate in the restaurant with a 270-degree view of the Sonoran Desert, backed by the majesty of the South Mountain…with 25 minutes until sunset. Such was the view that, after ensuring Sarah had chosen her location, Steven abandoned his inclination to sit in the corner, facing the floor of the restaurant, and sat at the obvious seat looking out over the theater that was surely the envy of the other restaurant patrons.

"Well, I guess timing is everything," offered Sarah as they arrived at the table, nodding to the view and descending sun.

Steven smiled graciously. "Here's to not letting it go to waste." He raised his glass, and the two toasted to their fortunate circumstance, as Steven thought to himself, "Now perform, you son of a bitch."

He rested his chin on his folded hands and gazed over the landscape that opened itself to him. His eyes moved from side to side, and he catalogued each color and contrast of the browns and greens, the sunlight and shadows.

"I know you've seen this view many times," he said quietly, "but I have not. And so, thank you for allowing me the opportunity. It truly is magnificent and something I would have never found on my own."

"Oh, I suppose I'm showing off a bit. I tend to save this particular spot for when I need to impress someone or, on occasion, myself. But when you and Peter got me to agree to dinner, I don't know, this seemed like it would serve me well…a bit self-serving, I admit."

"A little self-service never hurt anyone," Steven pointed out, testing her sensitivity. Sarah showed no acknowledgement of his comment. Rather than press the point, he offered, "We both thought we owed you a nice meal after making you the center of our childish game. We were a bit surprised you actually accepted, but we stopped talking as soon as we got the order. I am very happy you agreed. Whatever your reason may be, it is a privilege for me…and a loss for Peter. And believe me, I have no plans on cluing him in. This, to his detriment, will remain his loss. Unless, of course, you choose to invite him back."

"I can't see when that would happen. Part of the reason Marc treats me well is because he knows I never take him or his hospitality for granted. No, you'll just have to describe it for him."

"I'm sure he will hang on every word," said Steven, with more than a hint of sarcasm. "I hope you don't feel as though this was wasted on the likes of me."

"Oh, I'm sorry…of course not. It is a beautiful sight I feel privileged to see every time I can. And I am happy to see and hear others appreciate it just as much."

Steven tilted his head and studied Sarah with a quizzical smirk on his face. After a moment, he observed, "I'm not sure if I am slowly becoming a friend or if, because of your vocation, you say things like that out of habit."

She accepted his volley and returned, "Well, I sometimes find myself perplexed as well, and in those sorts of unsure situations, I tend to assume the safe bet...professional courtesy. That way, you stand a better chance of not offending me, and I won't feel the need to keep interpreting what you say."

"I see why you are so good at what you do. Thank you for that piece of counsel." Steven offered his glass, and Sarah met it with hers. "To professional courtesy and polite guests..."

"...Beautiful views, excellent food, and stimulating conversation," continued Sarah. Steven stopped himself from commenting on the word "stimulating." Sarah noticed.

In tune with her surroundings, Sarah did not resist the urge to gaze out at the captivating contrast that unfolded outside the corner window. The sun slowly descended between two mountain peaks, almost nestling there for a brief moment, before continuing its bow to the world below. As it dropped, shadows stretched over the landscape and poured over the illuminated green of the golf course that wound itself throughout the valley. The light became softer, even as those shadows pierced the surrendering colors of the fairways. Remarkably, it seemed a canvas was laying itself open to the hand of a master improving his work, where most would believe the scene to be in no need of additional tweaks.

At least, that is what Sarah saw. After joining her with a quick glance at nightfall, Steven spent the next several minutes congratulating himself on his patience as Sarah locked her eyes on something that happened yesterday and would happen again tomorrow. After a few more moments, when he could no longer see the golfers finishing their rounds, he'd had enough. "Amazing, wasn't it?" He proposed, shattering the silence and drawing Sarah back into her seat inside the restaurant.

"Hmm…oh, yes, it is. I got caught up. You would think by now it would have lost some of its shine…so to speak. But you only get to see it once, yeah?" She said as she sank backward, releasing her mind from where it had been.

"Once?" Questioned Steven. "That can't be. You have already admitted to sitting at this very table on many occasions. You've seen a ton of sunsets."

Sarah smiled, accepting his observation. She admonished herself for divulging a bit of her personal makeup. After all, it was merely minutes ago she had worked out the expectations for the evening. But as Steven squinted slightly in her direction, she knew he had not connected the thought behind her utterance. Maybe she could keep it that way.

"Oh, yes…of course you're right," she offered, hoping it would satisfy his need for an explanation. Alas, she quickly found it had not provided the clarity he sought.

"I know I'm right," he pressed. "What I don't know is why you said it. Clearly, you meant it. I must be missing something. Care to fill me in?"

Sarah raised her hands and twirled the ring on her right hand as she studied Steven and the situation for a moment. She realized this moment wouldn't pass until he got an explanation he could understand. She also quickly determined it wasn't important enough for her to dodge.

"OK. You're correct. I've sat at this table, in this chair, and have witnessed many sunsets through those windows."

"I'm with you so far."

"But that sunset only happened once. It was unique unto itself."

Steven didn't let his eyes leave Sarah's as he grinned. "You mean like this glass of water is unique? The next glass will be unique?"

Sarah breathed deeply, "No, I suppose not. Other than the ice melting, one glass of water is not necessarily different from the next. Just as changing the tablecloth on this table doesn't make it a different table."

"Then…"

Sarah continued, "What makes it different …to me…is that those things are static. But sunsets are comprised of a completely new set of circumstances with each dusk."

"Circumstances?"

"Circumstances…time of day, temperature, clouds, season…how many more would you like?"

Steven gestured with his hand that he understood, then surmised, "The sun comes up, and the sun goes down."

Sarah corrected, "Each sunset, Mr. Cross is a happening. Besides, how many people come to a restaurant to stare at their water glasses?"

Steven continued what he considered playful banter, "You're not a sun worshipper, are you? I mean, you have lived on the West Coast and now live in Phoenix."

Sarah decided quickly she would not shrink from his barb, "Not at all. I believe in one God…and I enjoy all His creations."

"Even me?"

"Even you. You must serve some purpose."

A moment passed before they both smiled, bemused by the exchange. But while Steven felt energized, Sarah felt expended.

"Do you go to mass?"

Sarah straightened a bit and quietly considered that at this stage of whatever relationship they were establishing, it was a question he could have little real interest in and was an answer she was not interested in providing.

Sarah reset her gaze at Steven and saw his eyes squint in recognition of the end of that particular subject.

She began again with a personal probe of her own. "So, tell me again why you and Peter came to Phoenix," she sipped her wine and waited.

Steven sipped his drink and contemplated his answer. He lowered his glass and shrugged, "A continuation of San Diego, I suppose."

"And what was it you were looking to continue?"

"Getting to know you better."

"Continuing the game you started in that pub…"

"Of sorts."

"Funny. Peter swears he's not playing anymore."

Steven squared his gaze at Sarah and decided he, too, would not flinch. "He's not," he plainly responded. "Really, he never was."

"Oh? Do tell," Sarah leaned in, feigning intrigue.

Steven leaned in and whispered, "I was playing for the chance to get to know you. Peter was playing for me not to get you."

Sarah raised her eyebrows slightly. She leaned back and conjectured, "Mr. Max is taken, is he? It's nice his wife lets him gallivant with you. Or is he along to keep you out of trouble?"

"Oh, you would have to believe a man must be either fully committed to another, or should be committed, not to have an interest in someone as beautiful as you," added Steven. It was Steven's turn to be dismissive, and he was enjoying it. "But...Oh, I don't know...Who can figure these things out?"

Sarah felt a bit uneasy that her immediate conclusion had shown a bit of vanity. But she also realized she had once again lumped Steven Cross and Peter Max together in like motives, and that was a mistake.

"Well, all's the better. It's probably good he doesn't find me attractive. I don't know if I have the strength to ward off both of you."

Steven leaned back as well, replying into his glass, "Oh, he finds you attractive, all right. That's why he's not here."

"Excuse me?" She asked, trying to process what she knew she had just heard.

"Hmm?"

"You just said Peter did not come with you because he *is*

attracted to me?"

"In a matter of speaking…"

"What, is he in seventh grade? Is he afraid to talk to girls?" Sarah's tone was becoming accusatory.

Steven raised his arms with palms out, then up, to fend off her questions. "Don't shoot the messenger. I can't figure it out either! But I certainly don't have any problem talking with beautiful women."

She accepted his attempt at cleverness, but her head bowed, and she stared at the plate in front of her for a moment. Something wasn't right. She couldn't let it go. As much as she didn't want to, she was about to get personal.

"Why?" she asked.

"Why what?" Steven asked back.

"Why isn't he here?" She insisted.

Steven first shifted his position in his chair, then the silverware, as if deciding if he should continue. He placed his elbows on the table, crossed his fingers, and lowered his face on top of them, still seemingly contemplating what to say next. Three, two, one…

Steven audibly breathed in, then confessed, "Our wives left us both in the same year. Same day, as a matter of fact." He let his breath escape as if relieved he was able to say it.

Sarah nodded her head in understanding and waited. When nothing followed, she let him know she needed more. "I'm sorry. That must have been hard for both of you. Were you close back then?"

"Very. The group spent most of our time together. The world was in front of us…we were young and successful for our age. We did what we wanted when we wanted." Steven's voice trailed off a bit as he continued, "But we took it for granted…We never saw it coming."

Sarah again nodded her head. This time she didn't wait long at all for Steven to continue.

"I think being caught off guard took the biggest toll on us," he continued. "We thought we were in control…of everything. Never missed a trick, you know? Looking back, it must have been arrogance to think that way. We sure got taught a lesson…shock to the system…swift justice, I suppose."

"I can hear in your voice how hard that must have been…for both of you," Sarah offered. "How did you and Peter get through it?"

"We both lived off the bottle for a while. Almost *died* from the bottle might be a better way of putting it."

"That's always a temporary solution."

"But, sometimes necessary."

Sarah cut to the chase, "Your friendship made it through, though."

Steven tapped his fingers on the table and gazed out into the darkness. "This trip is the first time we've been together, much less seen each other since they left."

Sarah gasped involuntarily, surprised at that revelation. "Oh, I wouldn't have guessed that…that's amazing to me…the way the two of you…" Before she could finish, another, more important question came to her. "How long ago was that?" She inquired.

Steven looked at her again, "Nine years ago…today."

CHAPTER 18

Peter sat upright at the top of the bed and swabbed a bit of egg yolk onto his lightly buttered toast while he perused the WSJ for news of the world. He admitted to himself that while this trip was not of his choosing, it had been therapeutic. He was pleased that his venture back into friendship with Steven had been much less awkward than he would have guessed, when the offer was made. Even more, he was a bit relieved he could still function outside the fortress of his gymnasium. He felt a bit freer. Time will allow for that, he concluded. But until this very morning, he would have argued against it.

His phone rang and he picked up before the second ring.

"Why is it," he began, "that you go out with her, and the next morning I get breakfast delivered to my room?"

"Wow. I'm better than I thought! No wait…I'm as good as I thought!" came the reply.

"Careful. You'll make me choke. It must have been something

you said, because I know it wasn't something you did."

"All in good time. What did the note say? You did get a note, right?"

Peter picked up the folded piece of paper that lay on the tray. *Peter, sorry you could not make it last evening. Although, I felt at times you were there. I hope the rest of your stay with us is as exciting as it is relaxing. Best, Sarah*.

"What does she mean by my being there at times?" He asked Steven pointedly.

"Not sure. I may have mentioned you at some point," Steven evenly replied.

"You wouldn't have asked about my note unless you wanted to share yours. Let's have it."

"What! Why would I want you to…OK…here it is: *Steven, Thanks for what turned out to be an extremely enjoyable and enlightening evening! It was indeed a "happening"! I'll look forward to seeing you again on Sunday! Best, Sarah*.

"Well done. I'd have laid even money we'd be forced to check out today. But today is only Thursday. Do you plan on staying here until Sunday?"

"Well, I'll have a room here, but I may not be staying here."

"Smart not to parade your prizes through the lobby or have

room service foil your plan with a slip of the tongue to upper management."

"Oh, Piper, c'mon…it's not like that," pronounced Steven.

"It's exactly like that," replied Peter, unbelieving.

"There are a lot of other things to experience in the Phoenix area. I may be too tired to make it back every night and just crash somewhere else."

"Uh-huh. And I guess you expect me to hang around through Sunday, too?"

"Well, you kinda have to."

"Go on," said Peter plainly, knowing his stock had just gone up.

"Relationships are a mysterious thing, you know. Sarah and I hit it off last night…I mean really broke through the ice. But the only way she agreed to spend more time together was if she gave us a tour of the desert…. both of us," explained Steven.

Peter laughed into the phone and extended it well beyond normal, only stopping briefly to yell, "You've met your match, my friend!"

Steven felt the need to defend himself. "It's all part of the plan…all part of the plan."

Peter sputtered his laughter and observed, "I didn't know you had plans that went past 24 hours."

"Whatever, jackass. What tee time did you get?"

"9:38…I'll meet you in the lobby at 9:15."

"Fine. But I'll meet you over there."

"Cool," replied Peter, and as the two men hung up, it occurred to him why Steven would not be using the lobby this morning. He didn't have anything to say, so it wasn't part of the plan to run into Sarah.

CHAPTER 19

Someone thought ahead when designing this place. Peter sat on the rear balcony of the Eagle's Nest Marriott and appreciated the layout of the terrace. Technically, it was the West balcony since he at once noticed the sun would come to rest in front of the post-golf/pool, current-cocktail, pre-dinner guests of the resort. But it went beyond that.

What earned the terrace exceptional marks was its design. Since he was thirteen years old, Peter had come to know his perspective when standing up was going to be different than most...his height would always allow him a line of sight more encompassing than average, even above average human beings. But he had also come to know that the differential between people when seated wasn't as significant. The view was similar for the most part, and therefore, impediments were the same for him as most others. That is why he took extra appreciation, in his current view.

Peter had turned his chair so he faced directly over the pool, into the green hedges, and up into the dimming sky that was deciding which colors to display next. As he sat with his right ankle rested upon his left knee, he lifted first his rocks glass, then his cigar to his lips and continued his stream of thought.

What made this view impressive was the natural progression of the scenery transitioning from day to night. However, it was delightful due to the foresight of the person who ensured that nothing they would do would take away from nature's evening performance. Peter was impressed with this person for a very simple reason: the protective barrier enclosing the terrace for the safety of the guests was made of glass. That allowed him to look down upon the pool area for the beauty of the water, gardens, and even some of the patrons. But, if the glass wasn't enough, instead of a wooden or metal rail that would artificially slice the horizon in half, the partitions were topped with three thin but formidable wire cables that were barely noticeable against the green shrubbery on the other side of the pool area. Finally, those cables were placed high enough to prevent any mishaps from impaired guests leaning or falling against them, but were also below the tree line, allowing the sky to be free of any impediments. He knew, just knew, that the designer sat in a similar chair, in a similar spot, to make sure these things were in place.

It wasn't what was meant to be noticed but rather what wasn't noticeable that Peter saw. As he sipped and smoked once more, he relished the fact that his mind was free enough to contemplate such

185

things.

"From the look on your face, it seems you are pleased with yourself," said Sarah softly from behind.

"Goodness," observed Peter, "you are a quiet one, aren't you? But, since you're back there, how can you see what expression is on my face?"

"Your face is reflected in the glass fencing," came her explanation.

Peter looked into the partition and saw Sarah's figure silhouetted within her dress by the hotel lighting. He didn't feel bad about holding his answer for a little longer than usual as his eyes took in another appreciative scene. "Very good, detective. Do you look into opponent's lenses when you play poker, too?"

"Why, I don't know what you mean?" She offered back sheepishly. "That would be cheating. Wouldn't it?"

"Well! Some would argue if the other player provides a resource, you would be well within your rights to use it." Peter decided he had used her reflection to his advantage long enough for decency and turned slightly, motioning to the chair beside him. "Would you like to sit for a moment, Sarah?"

"An invitation from Peter?" Observed Sarah, as she accepted the offer. "I was under the impression only Mr. Cross enjoyed my company."

"Mr. Cross enjoys company very much…me…not so much. I suppose you are to be congratulated once again for your observations." Peter held his cigar up. "Does this bother you?"

Sarah replied immediately, "Not at all. In fact, it would be a waste to extinguish such a fine cigar."

"Oh! I wasn't going to put it out. I was taking inventory of what I could use to end this conversation, if necessary." Peter grinned in her direction.

"Something tells me you don't have a problem ending conversations when necessary."

"Three for three," acknowledged Peter. "Confirmation of why you are superb at your job." When Peter stopped speaking, he looked at Sarah with a warm smile, and Sarah realized he had placed his defenses on hold, if only temporarily.

After a long pause, she also realized she was staring back at his warm smile. Peter broke the silence.

"I'm glad you stopped by. I did not want the day to pass without thanking you for breakfast this morning. Steven must have made me sound pretty good to get a free meal."

"However he made you sound, I did not want Steven thinking he had earned a breakfast all to himself."

Peter tipped his glass her way in appreciation of her insight.

Sarah nodded affirmatively and offered, "It's regrettable you couldn't join us last night."

"My apologies. I know it must have been an awkward situation keeping him at bay…" Peter tested the waters. "…unless just the two of you suits your tastes better?"

Sarah looked at him quizzically. "Now, Peter…I know you are much brighter than that," she said, scolding. "My powers of observation have alerted me to your powers of observation…and your powers of observation must have alerted you I am a willing participant with the two of you only until the situation becomes awkward. After that, you'll have to find a new player."

Peter responded plainly, "I already told you I'm not playing…"

"Not playing…I remember," interjected Sarah. "But just for the record…helping him play…makes you a player."

"And that makes you…?" requested Peter.

"Well, in San Diego, I was a prize," she retorted. "Now, I believe I've entered the game."

They stared at each other for a moment. She had added a bit of arrogance to the conversation. He knew she had as well, but he was wondering why.

"I can assure you, if you deemed me a player in San Diego, I won't spend any time arguing that, although our perspectives would differ. And if you are saying Steven is pressing on, I won't pretend or defend. But whatever my intentions were in San Diego, they remained inside that bar." Peter's face is too on a serious tone, not angry, dead serious, and convincing.

When he felt Sarah understood, Peter suddenly felt the need to stop the verbal chess match and drive home the point. "Besides, Steven doesn't need my help with those types of games," he started, as he raised the cigar toward his mouth in perfect chauvinist rhythm. "He usually fucks whoever he puts sets his sights on."

A moment of silence.

Then she burst out in laughter, bending slightly at the waist and rejecting his attempt at pigdom. Peter couldn't help but smile widely through the cigar clenched between his teeth. He had been called out. And he was enjoying it.

For Sarah, the last few minutes confirmed that Steven had been honest about something last night. Peter may have found her attractive, but he did not have an interest. She told herself that was the reason she felt more comfortable showing her personal, less cautious side to him.

The laughter subsided into intermittent chuckles.

Sarah continued, "You really were missed last night. It was actually quite enjoyable once we got the boundaries established."

"I think I would have enjoyed the boundary setting," reported Peter pleasantly. "I just didn't feel up to it."

Sarah tested again. "Bad memories will do that," she said flatly.

Peter looked up from his glass, alerted to her knowledge.

"Ahhhh…" he exclaimed with a sudden understanding. "So I was there in spirit anyway." He considered his next response for a moment. He usually would have shut down the conversation, this time for real and without any confusion. But oddly, something prevented him this time.

Sarah sat still and wondered if she had gone too far. Yesterday, it wouldn't have mattered. Twenty-four hours later, she may have touched a sore spot and she found herself caring.

"What did he tell you?" It was Peter's turn to tread deliberately. Being clued in was one thing…her intimate knowledge would be quite another.

She summed it up with regard for both Peter's privacy, as well as the mended friendship of the two men. "At some point in the evening, once we made it through the setting expectations part, he clarified you had taken time for yourself because it was the same day your wife left."

"My wife...*left?*" Inquired Peter, wanting to confirm the word she used.

"Yes, he mentioned both of your wives."

"Did he happen to say where she went?"

Sarah could sense she should have left the topic alone. Peter was measuring his words and his expression had become a bit more intense.

"No," she stated. "I shouldn't have mentioned it. I'm sorry. Steven didn't go into detail last night, and I certainly didn't feel it was my place to ask for specifics."

"Then why would you mention it?"

"I suppose I wanted to let you know I understood why you didn't join us last night. And I realize the toll divorce can take on someone. I wanted you to know...that I was thinking of you and wish you well.

"Have you ever been married?" asked Peter.

"No."

"Ever have someone leave you... alone...without warning?"

"I guess there must have been a time when -"

"And then, you realize it was your fault?"

"No."

"Do I seem like the kind of guy who would let a divorce affect me?"

"No." Sarah thought about that particular question again. Then, she offered her thoughts to Peter. "In truth, Peter…at the heart of what Steven told me last night was my appreciation for the fact that, at one time…you were in love with someone. And somehow, that person was able to hurt you with that love."

Peter studied her. He was impressed with her succinctness and that she was rarely off base. But he wanted to clarify something. "It wasn't her love that causes me pain…" Peter lifted his glass. "I'm afraid it was a self-inflicted wound. And every year, I prefer to wallow in remorse."

Sarah had placed herself in this position, and all she could think was how dark and anguished the conversation was becoming.

"Melissa's way of leaving me…was to die," Peter said in a low, matter-of-fact tone. He had decided right then and there that he wasn't going to be vague about the circumstances. If Sarah was going to know a little, she was going to know a lot. He didn't deserve vague. "That was my wife's name, Melissa."

"I see."

"How much do you want to know?"

"I'm not sure I should know any more."

"And I'm not concerned about what privileges you should or shouldn't have, or what depth of understanding you will have...all I'm concerned with is keeping you from your job or boring you."

Sarah thought for just a moment and offered, "As much as you'd like to tell me."

Peter had thought about the events in his mind so often they had become a stream of consciousness, called on at a moment's notice to be viewed silently again. However, when it had come time to put them forth in words, relay them to another, and put them in proper context, his thoughts ran together like the mixing of paint colors. His sudden realization of his inability to find a beginning to his story caused his fingers to rub his closed eyes in frustration as the search continued.

Sarah sat quietly and let him figure it out.

"Lisa," blurted Peter. And so it began. "Lisa was Steven's wife's name. She died, too."

"Ohh." Sarah's hand went to her mouth, and her eyes grew wide, as she remembered Steven saying the night before, "Our wives left us both in the same year. Same day, as a matter of fact."

"So, for this to make sense or be remotely informative, I should let you know a few things. Steven and I have been friends since our first year of high school. You know, at the start of freshman year, usually all the kids with last names that began with "C" and all the kids with last names that began with "M" would cling to each other and make friends, whether they like each other or not. Not with us. The way it worked out was I sat behind him in Biology…just the way the alphabet and number of students fell. We had a woman Biology teacher…with an abundant rear end. With our life changes going on and the subject matter coming from her mouth, we didn't know if we should laugh or walk with our books in front of us as we left. Come to find out, we had lunch at the same time, too. Just that quick, we were friends. I won't spend much time on this, but what made him my best friend was a single event…a clarifying show of support so small in its execution, yet immensely profound in its timing."

Peter stopped and directed, "Ask me what happened."

Sarah obliged. "What happened?"

"I got high and drank to the point where I wandered away from a party and laid on a stranger's front sidewalk until 3 a.m. When I finally made it back, Steven was still there waiting for me. He had left his ride home to wait for my sorry ass."

Sarah grinned, and Peter knew she didn't quite get it. But how could she? It was his moment.

"So, OK," Peter began again, "we became best friends, and

from the first day, that was never tested. All through high school, all through different colleges, through numerous girlfriends and teams, through good luck and bad decisions, through being broke to making our mark, we were best friends. There never was anything we considered or even acknowledged as an obstacle to that friendship. After college, we both took jobs at Xerox. I hated the work and the company, but we drove our success through our competitions and made it a game. We started in the copier and fax division. And man, could they churn the salespeople. Succeed, or you weren't around long…and not unlike most places, they told you to succeed but expected you to fail. Anyway, Steven and I didn't buy into that shit. We succeeded because we wanted to outperform the other. We performed so well we got moved to the printer division…you know, those high-speed behemoths that print for banks and insurance companies. Another country to conquer…and we did. It wasn't good enough to be the salesperson of the quarter…that was shit… salesperson of the year was the finish line. And if you didn't break the sales record…it didn't count. So, you know the progression for what were known as ambitious twenty-somethings, right? Long days, late nights, cutthroat sales turn into a large bankroll that becomes nice suits, nice cars, nice meals, nice condos, nice houses…not so nice women…mostly because nice women just don't fit this particular equation…"

"Am I supposed to be surprised that men are pigs, especially when they are young piglets?" bemused Sarah, cutting him off.

Peter had set the table for the rest of the story, and so he continued. "Then came Melissa."

Sarah's gaze became more alert.

"Steven met Lisa shortly after. We were soon a social foursome…see…still no obstacles to our life. We just changed the equations to accommodate the circumstances. It didn't matter that Melissa and Lisa didn't initially know each other. Steven and I would see to it that they would. I can't tell you how much I loved Melissa…you'll have to accept I loved her with everything I was. While she was here, I thought that would be enough, but for the man I was, it wasn't nearly enough."

Sarah instinctively felt the need to let Peter know she was listening. "Why do you say that?"

Peter half-smiled in her direction. "Well, here comes the pain."

Sarah couldn't help but shift in her chair a bit, as Peter paused to puff on his cigar and wet his throat with a prolonged sip of his drink.

"Melissa and I were married when we were 25. From the first time I can ever remember, I found myself thinking about her throughout the day and setting a time when my workdays would have to end, so I could spend every other minute with her. I actually planned vacation days. And I was so full of myself because I could do that and still beat my boy Steven when it came to sales numbers. We did what we wanted, when we wanted…and we wanted a lot. When we turned 30, we were still going strong…everything was bigger, and the prizes were still being accumulated. One Saturday, we had the Cross' over for a cookout slash game day feast…nothing strange…we did it all the time. Steven and Lisa show up; the guys open some bottles, retire to the patio, and then the basement to catch some of the game and listen to music. Every once in a while, we'd call up to make some sarcastic remark as our way of checking in with the wives. Afternoon turned into evening, and suddenly the grilled T-bones aren't sufficient for the guys anymore…we need lobster tails with them…and a nicer bottle of wine than the case I have on hand."

Peter brought the cigar to his mouth again and took a short-cut-off draw.

"Of course, the gents from the basement offer up that we've probably had a couple too many to make the trip, and besides, we needed to talk over the finishing touches to a deal we've been asked to negotiate…the deal's so big the company needs both of us in on it. Naturally, we should stay put and prepare the grill while they go on the errand…makes sense, right?"

Peter consciously kept the volume of his voice at a subdued level, but his staccato voice was becoming uneven. "Dutiful as ever, they went. It was two hours later when the cops interrupted us with a visit."

His head dropped slightly as he ended his sentence, and his eyes stared blankly at the label on his cigar. After only a few moments of silence, Sarah spoke up.

"Peter," she began, "that must have been a terrible time in your life. And I can understand you may have had some trouble coming to terms with the things you could have done better…" They both could hear the ending before she finished, but she said it anyway. "…but you aren't the first, nor the last person who misjudged the time we have with people who are close to us."

Without moving his head from its bowed position, Peter's eyes met hers. He exhaled a smirk and said, "Thanks. I know you mean that, and I've probably kept that part of the story within me much too long. And if it ended there, perhaps I'd agree. But I never tell that part, because it doesn't end there."

"No?"

"No. The last thing I said to my wife, as she was walking for the front door to leave, was to make sure she took our three-year-old daughter, Anna, with her…I couldn't be distracted from my conversation with Steven."

Peter shifted back in his chair and stiffened his spine. He would face this truth head-on.

"Of course," he continued, "We never spoke a word about the deal. I had just become too arrogant and too lazy to be put out. If it wasn't about me, it didn't matter. It wasn't important."

Sarah opened her mouth slightly, but Peter pressed on. "Now, I know freak things happen. This was not a smackdown from God, and I'm not looking for sympathy. But it happened…to me. I never considered a tragedy of this magnitude would be served up to me. I mean, what are the odds? Into every life, a little rain must fall, right? But come on. Who could or would expect something like that to happen? A car wreck? Ok. An injury? Sure. Lose my job…lose my hair…get fat…fall out of love…get cheated on…get robbed…get beat up. Life's not always fun and definitely not fair. I get it. No surprises here. I woke up nine years ago yesterday, and my life was gone. Oh…not in the strictest sense. I was still breathing, but I was stripped of the things I took for granted most when, in fact, they mattered most. And I never got the opportunity to see it coming…and protect…no…change. Instead, I was left with the thing that inflated my ego…my profession…my thankless, hollow, uncaring profession. And at the very moment I was left with it, I couldn't stand it. That putrid part of me was all I was. Did it really need to be that incredibly bad? Couldn't the lesson be learned some other way? I know I am ego-centric about it. My wife and daughter lost their lives. I lost them and kept my existence…that's why I believe this happened to me. It happened to me because I am so fucking stupid; I deserve to carry my grief and my guilt with me until I meet my end. It can never be painful enough or cause me enough anguish. If I let it go, I'd give myself another chance. That is a deal breaker. So, anyway…there it is, Sarah…A glimpse into my being."

Sarah asked, "Peter?"

Peter relinquished control of the conversation. "Yes?"

"With whom did you make this deal, that another chance would break it?"

"Me. As the story illustrates, it's always about me."

"What do you think your life would be like if they survived or if it never happened?"

"That's one of the few questions to which I contemplate the answer. And I suppose who can say? Steven and I would have won that deal, been promoted, and kept going…bigger, better, more expensive. Then again, life could have sent just the right message to wake me up and appreciate what I had."

"Really?" Sarah challenged.

Sure. Happened to Scrooge in one night…why not me?" Peter quipped.

"Well, I know you have spirits of the past. Believe me, we all do. Perhaps you need to find your spirits of the present and future."

"I don't live past the present," Peter blurted.

"Or maybe you're stuck in the past."

"It's a safe place to live. I won't put someone through that again."

"Ego-centric is how we all go through our experiences, Peter. There's nothing bad about that. But don't suddenly make your choices about saving others from terrible things. You're trying to save yourself from ever going through that again. And it truncates your life. Oh, and for someone focused only on himself, you just told me you wouldn't put another person through that again. Maybe you're not that ego-centric after all."

Peter stared quizzically at Sarah. It was the most he had ever spoken about his ordeal since the day it happened. Hell, he never even showed up for his grief counseling sessions. And she offered advice as if she had known him since childhood.

Sarah shrugged and raised the energy level a bit by adding, "Well, one woman's opinion…"

"How odd."

"My opinion?'

"That a woman would have one."

"Aaaand back to pigdom."

Peter and Sarah laughed softly, and each appreciated the effortlessness with which they left such a somber moment and moved on.

Sarah wiped imaginary debris from her lap and stood as she cleared her throat. "I must admit, I am now legitimately shirking my duties to the other guests."

"We all need to earn a buck. Perhaps I can warrant some time when you are off the clock."

"Is that your way of asking me out?

"Why, no. It's my way of trying to make you feel better for leaving me here an emotional mess," Peter feigned a pained expression.

"Somehow, I think you will be fine."

"Sarah?" Peter asked.

"Yes, Peter?"

"How did you know the answer to the question you asked me about where I'd be if my family hadn't died?'

Sarah paused. "It's a story for another time and pales in comparison to yours." She placed her hand on his shoulder, and he looked up at her. "But suffice to say, whatever skills I possess have been forged by some pain. I think we all contemplate our place in life…and sometimes through a lens of despair."

"Do you believe I'm desperate?"

"On the contrary. I believe you are one of the strongest people I've ever met. And I'm beginning to consider you a friend."

"Joy."

"And I believe you consider me one too."

Peter turned his chair back toward the edge of the terrace as Sarah exited. Now completely dark, the glass acted as a mirror, illuminating her figure beneath the dress as she walked toward the inside light.

"I can't compliment this glass fencing enough." He called out loudly enough so she could hear. "I had appreciated the view it allows looking out, but I'll also be sure to use it to watch for you coming toward me next time."

As she continued to walk toward the hotel entrance, Sarah replied, "Thanks…I had it installed last year."

Peter perused the fence and wire cables once more, then sat back in his chair and whispered to himself, "Funny…I thought for sure it would have been a man."

CHAPTER 20

S teven Cross spied the time on his phone, as he slipped through the side entrance of the hotel on the way to his room. 10:30…it was an acceptable time to sleep in… certainly nothing that would draw other speculation. Upon reaching his floor, he tilted his head carefully around the hallway corner. The housekeeping cart was three doors away from his, and the maid was not in sight. This would be the most important eight seconds of the day. Steven pulled his room key from his pocket and confirmed he had held it in the proper position. Taking a deep breath, he hustled down the corridor, reached his door, slid the key into the slot, and silently entered, while removing the Do Not Disturb door hanger he placed there last night before he left.

Once in, he walked to the bed, pulled down the comforter and sheet, and ruffled the pillows. For good measure, he walked into the bathroom, dampened a washcloth and towel, then threw both on the floor. He even unrolled the toilet paper and left two inches dangling from the spool. He flushed the paper and washed his hands clumsily over the sink, making sure to leave splotches of water on the counter.

Satisfied, Steven loudly opened his room door and allowed it to slam shut. He poked his head into the room three doors down and announced to the maid who was straightening the just-made bed, "Excuse me, young lady…I want you to know room 1218 is vacant and ready whenever you are." She smiled back and thanked him. Steven smiled back and placed a twenty-dollar bill on her cart. "And this is for your patience." Now, she smiled in earnest.

Steven pivoted and jaunted back down the hall. Upon exiting the elevator, he moved across the lobby, looking for two separate people. He didn't see either. He dialed Peter's number and spoke upon hearing, "Hey."

"I'm in the lobby. Where are you?"

"Vegas."

"Vegas?"

"Yeah."

"Then why am I in Phoenix?"

"Because you weren't in your room last night when I left."

"How did you get there? I've got the car, and the rental agency isn't open at night."

"The Bellman is $500 richer and without a motorcycle for a

couple of days."

Steven paused.

"Yes. That means I'll be back on Sunday for our fun day," confirmed Peter.

"So what am I supposed to do until you get back?"

"I'm sure you'll do someone…er, something."

"Actually, without you around, I can solidify my position with Sarah. By Sunday, the staff will consider me the greatest guest in the history of this resort. It can only get back to her. It will cost me, but I plan on making the ROI worth it."

"Well, you'd better get to work. It'll take a lot of cash to make that story believable."

"That's only because you know me too well," before Steven hung up, he had to ask the obvious. "By the way, why are you in Vegas?"

"I needed to be alone in a crowded city. What better place to be ignored than Vegas?"

"I guess that makes sense to you. Are you winning?"

"Yeah."

"It's going to be hard to stay anonymous if you force them to comp you."

"Too late for that, but I don't want the escorts to take note and spring into action."

"God forbid a lady or two pays attention to you."

"Not in the plan."

"OK, weirdo. Just be back by Sunday morning. I'm sure she'll have the day planned to the minute."

"I don't think she's thought about it since she invited us." Peter hoped saying it would convince him it was the case, although he knew differently. "I'll be there."

CHAPTER 21

Sunday morning room service mandated a full staff. Saturday night pre-orders could never be trusted. Whether induced by hangovers, forgetfulness, or spontaneity, everyone from line cooks to service staff knew the hours of 7:00 a.m. – 10:00 a.m. were hell. Lots of food prepared, and a lot of running, but little in tips. It was the nature of the beast, even at resort prices. Little in tips, unless, of course, you drew room 1218. Word had spread of the generosity of Mr. Steven Cross. Many would describe his generosity as extravagant or, better yet, exorbitant, and it had become the propellant for some kitchen wagering. The cook staff was excluded, given their effect on the results. Everyone else put $20 into a pan, and bets were placed on the lucky server. They would split the pot with their supporters.

Overall, delivery time was exceptional on this particular Sunday, as the wait staff practically threw trays at the guests who opened their doors. Oh, they would wait for their tips, but only with a nervous fidget. Some trotted down the hall, and others flat-out ran.

Elevators were abandoned for stairwells. After all, you could only get Cross' room if you were in the kitchen when his order came up.

"Order up!" bellowed the head chef as he placed a plate consisting of one egg and two pieces of toast on the warming shelf. Everyone's eyes were on Kate as she reached for the plate and placed it on her tray, glancing at the room number as she did so. As she spun on her heels and approached the kitchen's double doors, she stated matter-of-factly, "Split up the money in the pot and leave my half; I'm off to see the Wizard. This game is over, and I won't be serving anymore today."

As she made her way across the dining room, Kate could hear groans, F-bombs, and dropped trays. Room service standards dropped considerably for the rest of that particular Sunday.

Steven stood and critiqued his outfit in the floor-length mirror in his suite. He turned from side to side several times while keeping his head straight. After several seconds, he shrugged and asked, "What do you think?"

"I think you're funny," replied Kate from the bed.

"I mean about the outfit."

Kate wrapped herself in the sheet and approached Steven beside the mirror. Without speaking, she rested her head on his shoulder and smiled, as her hands reached around his waist and slowly un-tucked his shirt from his shorts. She then ran her hand up his right arm and with a quick tug, removed the tag from inside his sleeve.

"Thank you for your opinion. I'm glad you stayed."

"I'm glad you asked." Kate softly kissed Steven's neck, then retreated and placed her index finger across her lips while she stared into the mirror.

"What?" inquired Steven anxiously. "Is something missing?"

"Not at all. You look amazing," complimented Kate. "It's just...hmmm...something's not right."

"Is it the shirt? Too much for a casual afternoon?"

Kate didn't reply. After a couple more seconds, she removed her finger, walked to the room service tray, and removed the remnant of toast on the plate. She stood in front of Steven and kept eye contact as she lowered herself down his body. Once on her knees, she rubbed the toast across the front of Steven's new shoes, leaving a dark smudge on what was just pure white mesh. She did the same to his other foot and gently ran her fingers over both to massage the smudges. Satisfied with her work, she stood and kissed his lips. "Sometimes new...is just...too new. Now, you're ready."

Steven smiled and kissed Kate one last time. "Gotta love a

woman's touch. Thank you."

"You're welcome. What are we getting you ready for?"

"Oh, Sarah Garrity is giving me a personal tour of the desert today." Steven didn't feel the need to include Peter in his reply.

Kate's expression immediately showed her concern as she quickly stepped back from Steven. "Ms. Garrity?! You...you wouldn't tell her...you know...it's just I could get in trouble...I'm not supposed to..."

Steven smiled as he held Kate's shoulders. "Oh no...don't you worry about anything. Your extended visit stays in this room." Kate relaxed her shoulders and sighed with relief. Steven grasped her shoulders a bit tighter, causing Kate's eyes to engage with his. "...And I would appreciate it if you did the same," he requested. Kate nodded in confirmation.

Steven slid his hand up to Kate's cheek and caressed her skin gently. His eyes looked past her, to the discarded uniform on the floor. After spying her name tag, his eyes again locked with hers. "You certainly were a great start to my day, Kate. Feel free to stay as long as you like. Raid the mini bar if you want." Kate smiled. Steven separated and picked up his phone and wallet as he strode toward the door. He stopped abruptly and turned back as his hands instinctively opened his wallet. Kate quickly spoke, "You already tipped me for breakfast."

"I just thought maybe a little more…"

"No."

"No?"

"No."

Steven closed his wallet and exited the room, thinking how happy he was to be so close to the door, after that exchange. By the time he heard his door close behind him, his thoughts were on Sarah Garrity.

THOMAS K. SHANNON

CHAPTER 22

Steven stood silently. His mind wandered to a comment someone had made in conversation that the average person would wait three minutes before becoming frustrated, when waiting for an elevator. One of those "prove me wrong" asshole statements people make. He hated comments like that. Personally, he became frustrated after waiting fifteen seconds. Six elevators, and he still had to wait. He'd be sure to mention it to the general manager of this dump. Steven smiled, enjoying his humor. He could hear the elevator dings above and below him and wondered what was going on.

Just then, two young boys broke his concentration when they turned the hallway corner and pushed each other against the wall, as they screamed just for fun. The boys' mother entered the elevator space next, pleading, "Billy! Tommy! Please stop and behave! I'm in no mood for this! We have a long day ahead of us. C'mon! Please?!" The boys stopped screaming, but the pushing continued.

Their father turned the corner, pressed the already red call button, and shut his boys down with three words. "Knock it off!" he bellowed without turning around. The father stared at the elevator doors as if trying to open them with his mind. Steven heard more dings on other floors.

"What the hell is going on?!" he thought to himself. "This sucks!"

Not only was he waiting for an elevator, but he was now waiting with the stereotypically dysfunctional family of four. Worse yet, selling all those years in skyscrapers caused Steven to understand there was no such thing as elevator etiquette. He had spent enough time in office buildings and hotels to know if there was more than one elevator, whichever door opened first, the people closest to that door entered first. Fuck the people who were there before the others. It didn't matter. Even if they missed the elevator because it was full! Fuck them. They would have to catch the next one. So now, as the father stared at one set of doors, Steven was watching the other five, waiting for the ding and watching the gap at the bottom of the doors, watching for any change in the small line of light that would alert him to an arriving car. "Ding!"

Steven exhaled loudly as the light next to the father lit up, and his family huddled around him in Pavlovian fashion. In an instant, they had formed a mini phalanx! The doors opened, and Steven exhaled whatever he had left in his lungs. The car was full of people wearing Western gear, and for the first time, he realized the entire phalanx family was dressed like cowboys (and a cowgirl), too. What the hell was going on here?! The people in the car pressed themselves back, and the mini phalanx stepped as one onto the elevator and turned to face Steven. The mother smiled as the doors closed, reassuringly offering, "I'm sure there will be another one along soon."

As the doors came together and his reflection stared back at him, he finished her message, "Fuck you."

Steven turned and made his way to the stairwell.

As he turned the final corner, Steven accelerated down the final half-flight of steps and burst through what he thought was the lobby. By the time he realized the stairwell emptied onto the hotel's side parking lot, the door was closing fast behind him. It slammed shut, leaving him to stare at its dull gray paint. "Fuck me! Fuck me! Fuck me!" he exclaimed as he turned around in disgust, stamping his feet on the pavement for self-therapy.

Steven stopped abruptly and consciously inhaled and exhaled deeply as he composed himself. He symbolically pushed the air out with his arms as he breathed out. Satisfied he had regained his composure, he defiantly marched the length of the building toward the hotel's main entrance.

As the motion detectors activated and slid the doors sideways, he was immediately struck by the buzz of over one hundred people standing in the lobby. The second thing he noticed was that everyone was dressed in some sort of Western clothing. As he strode across the floor, he couldn't help but stare from person to person, trying to figure out what was happening. His head turned to the right, then back to the left as he walked. The final thing he noticed was the hoards of people were also walking about, looking at each other with great interest and quizzical looks. It dawned on him they were looking for others with the same color bandana. The buzz was caused by people finding others and making conversation, as they formed their same-color bandana groups.

As Steven was piecing all this together with continued bewilderment, he veered off course and knocked shoulders with a large man introducing himself to his new group of navy bandanas. The collision stopped Steven in his tracks, while the stranger quickly switched from cordial introduction to enflamed defenses.

"What the hell!" he exclaimed as he swiveled his head like a turret and peered at the intruder of his space. Steven bounced back a couple of steps, then steadied himself. His hands quickly brushed the large man's shoulder as he reassured, "My bad, my bad. I'm so sorry. I apologize. It was all me, man. My bad." He continued the brushing actions, even as he moved past arm's length. When he was comfortably in front of him, he turned to face front with a look of relieved terror, having just escaped physical retaliation. His eyes focused ahead and found Sarah Garrity giggling at him, as she leaned against the concierge desk with her legs crossed at the ankles.

She, too, was dressed in western attire. Steven had about forty feet to take her in, and he did so with great interest. "Damn," he thought, "She can even rock that look." He started with her brown boots that were functional yet feminine. Her jeans showed some age with faded areas around the knee and thigh, and that might have contributed to why they fit her so well. Her brown leather belt connected to a silver buckle with a touch of turquoise in the center. A canvas-colored shirt buttoned down the middle, showed off the purple bandana tied perfectly around her neck and slightly adjusted toward the left. Her arms rested beside her exceptional figure and her hands held a light brown suede cowboy hat and two white oversized envelopes. As he closed the final distance, he was able to make out "Steven Cross" and "Peter Max" handwritten on the front panels. Without looking down, she raised the appropriate envelope in front of her, and her chuckling turned into a welcoming smile.

Steven smiled back at her and accepted the envelope humbly. "I sure hope there's a purple bandana in here." He opened the envelope and dramatically wiped his brow in mock relief with the purple piece of cloth. "I don't have any idea what is going on, but at least I'll be in the right group." He peered down at Peter Max's envelope and said, half-kidding, "Can't we just make him green or something?"

Sarah shook her head no as she answered, "And break up the winning team? And my bodyguard? No, we'll all be joining forces today."

"So be it." Steven looked around again. "Where is Mr. Social, anyway? Can't wait 'til he gets a load of this."

Sarah's hand rose again with Peter's envelope extended, and Peter accepted it graciously with a smile but no words, as he finished his approach toward the Concierge desk. He let the envelope drop to his side. There was no reason to open it. He was already wearing a purple bandana tied around his bicep. He was dressed in boots, jeans, western-style button-down shirt, and he held a black Stetson in his other hand. He looked from Sarah to Steven, and his first words were, "Nice outfit. Are you going to a garden party?"

Sarah didn't mean to be rude, but before she could think, she burst out laughing and caught herself just in time to console Steven. "Ohhhh, how awful of me! I'm sorry. Peter's remark caught me off guard, and I laughed. But I didn't mean to laugh so hard!"

"Yeah, he's a real cut-up," deadpanned Steven. "What's going on here? How come you already have a purple bandana?"

Peter stared at his bicep and explained, "Since I knew we would be spending the day together, I asked the concierge yesterday what Ms. Garrity enjoyed doing on Sundays when she was off. He told me he didn't know because she wasn't off on Sunday. He informed me she was hosting the highly entertaining desert scavenger hunt for the hotel's guests. A few more questions and a nice tip later, he was kind enough to provide me with the bandana of choice for Ms. Garrity."

"And the get-up?" questioned Steven. "You don't own any Western stuff."

"Bill from Concierge is roughly the same size as me. He generously lent me his boots and hat, and I generously thanked him," replied Peter.

"Well, what am I supposed to do? I don't have any Western shit, and I haven't made friends with the people who work here," protested Steven.

Peter started, "At least no one who wears the same size…"

Sarah cut him off without absorbing his words and offered, "Oh, you'll be fine. You may even be more comfortable in that. Your shoes may get a bit dirty, though. I hope they aren't too new."

Steven quickly replied as he stared down at his feet, "New? Not at all. These things? Had them for a while."

"Well then," said Sarah as she pushed herself from the desk, "we just have to find the rest of our team, and we'll be all set."

"The rest…what? Asked Steven, realizing he would have to share Sarah with more than just Peter.

"Oh, good…here they come now," said Sarah.

Steven turned to see the family from the elevator approaching the Concierge desk, all with purple bandanas. It was his turn to react before thinking. All that came out of his mouth as they came toward him was, "Fuck me!"

CHAPTER 23

S teven immediately knew what he had said, and his right hand immediately cupped his mouth as he turned back wide-eyed to Sarah and Peter.

Peter smiled broadly as Sarah questioned, "Why, Mr. Cross, are you OK with children?"

Steven let his hand drop. "Of course, of course. The boys just remind me of my nephews back home. The resemblance is uncanny, truly."

Peter's smile grew wider.

"Good morning to the Phoebus family!" Sarah stepped toward the approaching brood and crouched to look directly into the hellions' eyes. "Well, you must be Tommy," she addressed the taller boy extending her hand holding a shiny Sheriff's badge." Tommy's arm swung wildly to swipe the badge from her hand. Sarah pulled it back as his chubby fist passed by. "Now, one thing you need to know," she explained. "Being a sheriff in Phoenix means you accept the responsibilities that come with the job."

She turned her glance toward the other boy without hesitation. "And I happen to have another Sheriff's badge for you, too, Billy." She opened both palms to display the gifts. Tommy and Billy stared at the badges but knew better than to take them before Sarah said it was okay. They knew she was too quick for them.

"For me to allow you to wear these badges, you both need to take an oath. Are you okay with that?"

The boys nodded.

"First, in these parts, a sheriff must speak clearly and with meaning. And he is polite. He usually ends a sentence with ma'am or sir. Can you do that?"

"Yeah!" exclaimed Billy, who was then elbowed by Tommy.

"Yes, ma'am," offered Tommy.

"That's it, Tommy. Billy?"

"Yes, ma'am," said Billy, catching on.

"Good. Now, sheriffs must look out for the rest of the team and make sure everyone stays together. That means if you see someone wandering off or not paying attention, you need to bring them back to the group." Sarah stopped abruptly and glanced at each boy twice. "Oh, boy...maybe that's asking too much of you. I mean that last one isn't easy, you know? That's just too much." Sarah began to close her hands and stand up, but Billy and Tommy were having none of it.

"No, no. We'll do it, we'll do it!" They looked at each other and then back to Sarah. They finished in unison, "ma'am!"

"All right then!" Sarah bent again and pinned a badge to each boy's vest. "It's official. I feel safer already." The boys beamed with delight.

Sarah stood and extended her hand toward the parents. Hello, Mr. and Mrs. Phoebus. I'm Sarah Garrity, and I'm very pleased you could join us today."

"Rose and Tom, please," offered Mrs. Phoebus. "Why, we're just thrilled to be on your team. We feel very special." Tom Phoebus stood with his jaw open a bit, impressed with how Sarah had just conquered his boys.

"Thank you, but please relax and enjoy yourselves. This is a treat for me to meet the resort's guests." Sarah turned and walked back to the counter where Peter was leaning.

"Never unprepared, are you?" Peter whispered as she gathered her things.

"Forewarned is more like it. The little ones have earned quite a reputation during their stay. Best to keep 'em close." Sarah confirmed. Knowing Steven was also listening, she added, "It's going to be a treat watching all of you interact."

Sarah grabbed Peter and Steven by their elbows and stepped a few feet forward again. "And may I introduce Peter Max and Steven Cross." Peter shook hands and smiled with Rose and Tom. Steven followed suit, and when he shook Rose's hand, she recognized him and gleefully reported, "You're the man who missed the elevator! I'm so glad you and your partner made it to the lobby!"

"Partner?" Steven recoiled.

"Oh, I'm sorry. Is that not the PC thing to say," offered Rose.

"I don't know if it is or isn't. But in this case, it's inaccurate."

"Yes, Steven is right. He doesn't consider anyone his partner," interjected Peter. "He'd much rather be known as the boss."

Rose laughed awkwardly, as her husband's face blushed with embarrassment. "Oh me, I shouldn't have assumed."

"No worries," soothed Peter. "Sadly, I wasn't there to help him get dressed."

Rose broadened her smile, realizing she was back on solid footing.

Sarah took the occasion to move things along and motioned to the activities coordinator. On cue, the coordinator started the day's events by playing the theme from the Lone Ranger. The crowd became quiet and attentive. The coordinator explained very simply that twelve teams of seven or eight guests would exit the hotel and find a custom jeep bearing their bandana color, a tour guide, and a packet of instructions waiting for them in the parking lot.

The day would end in about 2 ½ hours at an Old West-themed bar-b-q at a nearby ranch.

"With that, away you go!" she exclaimed.

The crowd dispersed in a sprint toward the parking lot.

It didn't take three seconds before Tommy barked out in Steven's direction, "C'mon dude, you're holding us up!" Steven pushed away reluctantly from the counter.

Sarah quickly corrected Tommy, "Politely, Tommy."

Tommy waved his arms excitedly toward the lobby exit, "You're holding us up, sir!"

Steven exhaled deeply as he shoved his bandana into his back pocket and sauntered toward the revolving door.

"Shotgun!" shouted Peter, enjoying the entire scene before him.

Outside, the custom jeeps were lined back-to-back down the hotel's driveway, facing the exit. Colored bandanas were tied to each vehicle's antennae, and an authentically attired Western tour guide stood by their team jeep with a poster board adorned with a colored bandana. Still, Peter witnessed frantic participants approach random jeeps demanding, "Where is the yellow bandana team going!?" or, "I don't see a red bandana! Are you sure there is a red bandana jeep!" As he saw the guides keep their smiles while pointing to a handy sheet with each Jeep identified by color and number, he couldn't help but conclude that the host company placed its most understanding and helpful tour guides closest to the hotel.

Peter continued his walk down the driveway and spied the purple bandana tied to the Jeep about four vehicles away in the middle of the pack. Behind him, he could hear the little Phoebus monsters running side by side, their sneakers clapping against the asphalt. He turned back to face them and shrugged his shoulders as he bent to address them. "Can't seem to find our Jeep, sheriffs. I'll need to follow you so I don't hold us up."

"Follow us, mister. C'mon!" screamed Tommy as he brushed past Peter. Billy brushed by on the other side and offered, "Can't you see our flag!? We're only four cars away!" Peter swung on his heels while crouched and watched the hellions push each other as they ran side by side.

"Yeah, come on, mister!" cajoled Sarah as she gently touched his shoulder as if to help him up. "Don't worry," she continued, "we won't let you get lost."

"Thank you, ma'am," Peter said as he rose, tipping his hat. "A greenhorn like me may need some tendin' to."

"I'll let the sheriffs know." Sarah kept walking. She smiled as soon as she knew Peter couldn't see her do it.

With that, Peter felt an open palm slap his shoulder from behind. "Where did that come from?" Steven insisted. "First time you've done more than grunt at a woman on this trip."

Peter quickly offered, "Just in the moment...dickhead."

"Yeah, well, be a pal and get to know the Phoebus family, will ya?"

"But they've already met you."

"They suck."

Peter and Steven arrived at the Jeep to find Billy and Tommy in the first row of seats behind the driver and Rose and Tom Phoebus behind them with Sarah. Without breaking stride, Peter slid into the front passenger seat and picked up the large manila envelope.

The guide for the purple bandannas looked over at Peter and welcomed him. "I see you are volunteering to be team captain. I'm Roger." He extended his hand.

Peter shook his hand. "Peter. What's that about team captain?"

"Very important. You call the shots."

Steven was still standing outside of the car, looking at the empty seat next to the Sheriffs, who continued to shove and elbow each other. "Wouldn't you two rather ride with your parents?"

Tommy looked up at Steven. "No way! Get in. You're slowing us down!"

"Slowing us down, sir," corrected Sarah from behind.

"Sir." Tommy threw in.

Steven climbed aboard. That was the cue for Roger to address the troops. He turned and faced the seated passengers. "Good morning, folks. I'm Roger, and I'll be your guide for what should be a fun day. Peter here has accepted the job of team captain, so he'll be the go-to guy when it comes to final decisions."

'Why is he the captain?" interrupted Billy. He immediately added, "Sir."

"Because he sat in the front seat, and he now has the envelope that holds the instructions for our day in the desert." Roger noticed Billy's badge and continued, 'Besides, you'll be too busy being a sheriff. That's a lot of responsibility."

Billy slumped back in his seat.

"Now, Peter will find a booklet in his envelope that explains the particulars, but there is one rule for the people in my Jeep that I will relay. That rule is, don't take the desert for granted. It is beautiful but demands your respect. It can go from fun to scary in an instant. Now, we have two sheriffs and a team captain on board.

Hopefully, I'm just the driver and a guide. But, if I speak up, you will do as I say…no questions. When I speak, I have rank. Agreed?"

The group responded with an assortment of ways to express agreement.

Yep. Okay.

Yessir.

Gotcha.

Sounds good.

No problem.

Whatever.

Satisfied when he received responses from everyone, Roger swung his arm toward Peter and introduced him. "*Vaqueras y vaqueros*, I give you Peter, the team captain. Peter, please fill your team in on today's challenge."

"Howdy. My name is Peter, and having been late to the Jeep, I am now your team captain. Now, by team captain, I mean the guy who reads to you. The rest of this expedition will be done by democratic vote. Your input is not only expected, but also required." Peter didn't feel the need to ask for agreement. It was a statement of fact. So, from the directions in this envelope, Roger will escort us into our assigned section of the desert to discover its wonders and do some interactive learning. As we visit different areas, we will gather certain things particular to that area like a scavenger hunt. And, in some places we will take team pictures and forward them back to headquarters. After we are done, we'll meet back at the ranch for some marksmanship and grub. The winning team will be judged on items collected, picture creativity, and time."

"Time!" squealed Billy. "Some Jeeps already left! We're already screwed!"

"Relax, sheriff." calmed Roger. Each Jeep keeps its own time. Our time will start when I hit the button on this here clock on my dash."

Steven used Billy's reaction as a teachable moment. "So, today will go much smoother if we all don't overreact or spout off without all the facts. We have the best darn team captain in the entire Old West. I'll trust his judgment, and so should you." Steven finished his sentence, looking directly at Billy while pushing his index finger into the loudmouth's shoulder. Billy swiped it away and yelled, "Hey! Owwww!!"

Steven turned toward the passenger window and softly condemned, "Wuss."

"Now, children..." corrected a smiling Sarah from behind Steven, "we are all part of a team, and we have a lot to do. This will be a lot easier and more fun if everyone gets along."

Steven began to speak up, but Sarah cut him off. "And acts their age."

Steven shut his mouth and slumped dejectedly against the passenger door.

"So, Captain Pete, are we ready, or do you have other instructions?" Sarah inquired toward the front of the Jeep.

Peter started his sarcastic reply, "No...Sa..." but got stuck before his second word. "I just realized there is not a shorter version of Sarah to insult you with...with which to insult you." He quickly corrected his grammar as he saw Sarah formulating her response about ending sentences with prepositions. She smirked at Peter's self-correction. He continued, "Well then, missy, I'll have to keep thinking about a name for you. Roger, how far to our first stop?"

"Approximately fifteen minutes, Cap'n Pete," answered Roger dutifully. Steven laughed loudly as he exclaimed, "I think that's gonna stick, Cap'n Pete!" Peter looked back at Steven in mock disgust but immediately focused on the broad smile on Sarah's face, showing most of her front teeth, very white and straight, encased by well-proportioned, subtly glossed lips.

All that came to him was, "How quickly things change." Peter turned back to face the front of the Jeep and, while doing so, slapped the back of Roger's seat with his left arm, causing the driver to lurch forward. "Let's hit that timer and get a move on!" commanded Peter.

"The ride will give me time to sort through the rest of these instructions and plan our strategy."

Roger reached toward the timer, but before hitting it, he asked Peter, "What about the team name?"

Peter continued to stare off into the distance. "I'll think of something….captain's choice, ya know. Got it…The princess, a rock, and a crown."

==

After three stops in 90 minutes, and a rising thermometer, the sheriffs were restless.

"This is stupid," blurted Billy.

Tommy chimed in, "Yeah, this is stupid."

In rhythm, "We wanna go to the pool!"

Steven shot a glance toward Mr. Phoebus that suggested he cut them off. Tom Sr. obliged. "Now, listen up! I don't wanna hear any back-talk from you two. We're all stuck out here together, and you need to suck it up with the rest of us!"

Steven looked awkwardly at Tom and asked, "Accountant?"

Tom shrugged his shoulders and responded, "I teach middle school."

Rose tried to be helpful and sweetly interjected, "Now, boys, let's enjoy ourselves with these nice people, and when we get back, we'll get some ice cream."

"Ice cream!" shouted Billy, as he jumped and turned in circles like a stuck pig.

"That's the button," Peter commented out of the side of his mouth toward Sarah, who couldn't decide whether to laugh or take control.

"I don't want ice cream," contributed Tommy. His mother smiled anxiously at her little cherub. "I want a milkshake!" And he joined his brother in the un-choreographed histrionics.

"This is like the brat Olympics," observed Steven, as he strode past Tom Sr., patting his shoulder.

Spurred by Steven's comment, the boy's father stepped forward with his hand outstretched. "Stop right there! You're going to get sweaty and thirsty, and I'm not going to give you anything to drink!"

The boys responded with their loudest scream yet.

Sarah stepped forward, knowing she was out of her league. "Now, sheriffs," she started with her arms waving in a calming motion. "We are just about to start the most treacherous part of this journey, and we will need both of you to help us make it through."

The boys continued jumping and had now joined arms, facing

each other.

Peter walked quickly past Sarah toward the Jeep. As he passed the boys, he announced, "All right, ice cream and pool it is!"

The boys snapped back to reality and attention and looked at Peter for confirmation. "That's right," Peter turned back to face the boys after hearing the shouting stop. As he shuffled slowly backwards, he continued, "As team captain, I decree this scavenger hunt complete…well, not complete…but done. The boys are right, what more can we see out here anyway? I mean, we've seen brown dirt, brown plants, and loads of cactuses… Owwww!" Peter suddenly grabbed his ankle and fell to the ground. As he rolled over, he stretched out his hand in an attempt to grab something that was out of his reach. He rolled back and caught the boy's stares. "Owww! It got me, sheriffs!"

"What got you?!" asked a stunned Rose.

Peter winced loudly, then glared back at Rose. "Scorpion. The big black kind, too."

Roger stepped forward confidently, "Okay, everybody… everything's just fine. From Cap'n Pete's description, he will be fine. You see, the darker the scorpion…"

"The longer we have to find an antidote!" Sarah exclaimed.

"Antidote?" questioned Roger. "He don't need no-" In mid-sentence, Roger finally caught onto what Peter and Sarah were up to. "Ohh, the antidote…yes…"

Steven strode purposely toward his friend, but as he passed in front of the brothers, Peter lifted his hand from his ankle, made the OK sign, and smiled, stopping Steven in his tracks. He peeled off and continued toward the Jeep, saying, "I'll look for a first aid kit."

"Good, Mr. Cross, that will come in handy." approved Sarah. She turned towards the mesmerized boys and squatted between them. "But that will only stall the inevitable. We must find some antidote as soon as we can."

"But where?" asked Tommy quietly.

"Out there." Sarah pointed further into the desert.

"Why don't we take him to a hospital?" questioned Rose. Sarah's head dipped a bit in frustration.

"Because, little lady," Roger educated her with a wink, "hospitals don't have scorpion antidote. We make that from things found in the desert."

"Ohhhh…" said Tom Sr., finally catching on and squeezing his wife's shoulders.

"What happens to him if we don't find the antidote?" required Billy. "Does he die?"

Sarah and Peter looked at one another for a moment. Peter

expanded his hands over his imaginary wound.

"No," consoled Sarah. "His foot will just swell up and pop like a balloon."

"Cooool.", imagined Tommy.

Steven arrived at Peter with the first aid kit and administered bug spray on Peter's ankle. Peter jumped up and began walking with a slight limp.

"How much time do I have, Roger?

"Oh, I'd say another 90 minutes."

"Perfect." That gives us time to find an antidote and complete the scavenger hunt!"

"Just so happens, all of the ingredients we need to make an antidote are on our way to the campground."

"Isn't that convenient," stated Steven, faking astonishment. Sarah shoved him playfully on his shoulder, as she escorted the Phoebus family toward the Jeep. Steven glanced at his shoulder, then Peter, then back at his shoulder.

"Good for you," Peter said smartly as he also walked past with his ever-so-slight limp.

As they all approached the Jeep and configured themselves within the vehicle, Steven couldn't help but point out, "Well, Cap'n

Pete, I sure am glad you're going to be okay…that is, if we find you the stuff we need for an antidote. But I just wanted to ensure the boys here don't learn incorrect things on this here scavenger hunt. After all, it is supposed to be a learning experience."

"I'm sure we are all ready to be educated," prodded Peter.

"Well, in the whole scheme of things, it's a small correction, and given your scorpion bite, I'm hesitant to even mention it…" He turned a bit more toward Sarah to make sure she was listening.

"Go on," prodded Peter.

"You said 'cactuses,'" Steven paused. "Actually, the plural of cactus is cacti." Steven shut his passenger door tightly.

"Actually…," from behind him, he heard Rose volunteer as she leaned forward toward her children, "Actually, the plural of the same species of cactus is cacti. The plural of cactus when referring to multiple species is cactuses. So, Cap'n Pete was correct if that was what he was describing."

"And scorpions don't bite…they sting," added Tom Sr., mimicking his wife's gesture.

Sarah fell back into her driver's side corner with her purple kerchief up to her mouth. Peter shut his passenger door tightly.

"Off we go, then." Steven petitioned of Roger.

"Ready, Cap'n?" asked Roger.

"If he says so," responded Peter, pointing back toward Steven. As he returned to the front of the Jeep, he again halted momentarily at the sight of Sarah, as she smiled silently in approval.

By the time the purple bandanas made their way to the finish line at the ranch, Peter's ankle had been swabbed with all sorts of berries and cactus-produced aloe, then wrapped tightly for effect. The sheriffs had been conned into constructing a makeshift crutch from two pieces of deadwood and some vines.

As the team approached the other tour guides, who had arrived earlier, they asked, "What happened? Are you alright, sir? Rog, how come you didn't radio us about an injury?"

Peter limped passed, reassuring them, "Relax, fellas, nothing two more minutes, 100 yards, and three beers won't cure." Spying a wooden bench, Peter's last duty as captain was to close the envelope containing their scavenger hunt results and scribble the team name on the front. He then gestured the two boys toward him. "Sheriffs, this envelope needs to be delivered to the head table inside those gates. The team needs you again. I'm entrusting this envelope to you. Be sure no one takes it from you until you reach the final drop-off. Okay?"

"Yessir.", snapped back Tommy.

"Now, run as fast as you can so we can beat the others."

The boys literally left in a cloud of dust.

"Aaaand that's a wrap," announced Peter, unwrapping the bandage from his ankle.

"That was a stroke of genius, Cap'n Pete," complimented Tom Sr. "I should have thought of that. I'll sure use it when we get back home. Shoot, I'm gonna use it on my middle school students."

"Careful," warned Peter. "You start faking stuff, people will eventually call you on it."

"But it came so naturally to you," interjected Steven.

"I was in sales at one time. In fact, I was number one in sales, if you remember."

"Like riding a bike, huh?"

"Kinda. More like knowing your customer. The sheriffs were acting just like purchasing agents, so I just distracted their attention off the price." Peter stood and shot the rolled-up bandage into a trash can ten feet away. "Nowadays, I only have to be straight with my players. They don't need distractions from their goals. In fact, I have to keep them from thinking about their distractions, if you know what I mean."

"Oh, I think I know."

"Yes, you do."

Peter hopped toward Sarah, keeping his bare foot from touching the ground. When he arrived at her side, he touched her shoulder and asked humbly, "Would you mind lending some support back to the Jeep so I can get my shoe?" Without thought, Sarah placed her arm around Peter's waist, and walked him toward the Jeep. As they walked/hopped away, Peter turned his palm skyward as Steven looked on.

"Good for you." exhaled Steven as he sat on the wooden bench.

==

Peter arrived at the picnic table with three more cups of beer and placed them in front of Steven and Sarah, as they laughed while spying the sheriffs, painting their faces with ice cream cones that were too big for their mouths. "Kind of squashes the motherly instinct, doesn't it?" Steven offered, glancing at Sarah.

She changed her expression slightly, as the comment resonated more with Peter's story than with her own single status. She glanced at Peter as he sat back down next to Steven. Seemingly, the remark had no effect. "No," she responded. "It just reminds me they eventually become men."

Peter laughed out loud. "No one ever said men were hard to figure out."

"Actually," she countered, "Eighty percent of a man is easy to figure out. It's the other twenty that gives women fits."

"I can guess the contents of the eighty percent," said Steven as he brought the fresh beer to his mouth. "What's in the other twenty?"

"Oh, that's where honor, integrity, and accountability reside," explained Sarah, as if she had considered this deeply. "The problem is, it's also where ambition and imagination can be found. The wrong mixture can make for one fucked up individual."

Steven shifted his eyes, contemplating the equation.

"And what of love? Where can that be found?" questioned Peter, making eye contact.

Sarah quickly smiled and just as quickly responded, "Well, in my estimation, a man feels love when lust is drawn from the eighty percent and transfigured by the qualities of the twenty percent."

"And a woman?"

"Women? Well, isn't that the age-old question?"

"Sure is," interjected Steven, in an effort to stay in the conversation.

"It's only an old question because women refuse to answer it," Peter dared.

Sarah took a drink from her cup and placed it on the table deliberately. She again met Peter's gaze and said simply, "Women have the same eighty/twenty split. But with women, love is always a part of the twenty. We don't need to be convinced to love. We just need to protect ourselves from the men for whom lust never makes the transition."

All three took a drink from their cups.

"Well, that may be, but it's too deep for me," quipped Steven. "But I've come across plenty of women who act an awful lot like men."

"I didn't say women always get the measurements right. We can be just as fucked up as any man."

"Here, here!" cheered Peter.

"Hell yes, here, here!" joined Steven.

Sarah shook her head in amusement. "Here, here," she surrendered.

They sat quietly for several seconds until the announcements started from the stage. "Ladies and gentlemen, cowboys and cowgirls, may I have your attention," boomed the voice from the microphone. "Everyone at the Double R Bar ranch hopes you enjoyed your day in the desert and the grub and suds afterwards." He paused, and the entire group offered applause. "You have been a great group of hunters, and the contest was very close. We have tallied the scores, and I have to tell you, for the first time in a long time, we have a tie for first place!"

The crowd offered its appropriate gasps of surprise.

The announcer continued, "Let me first congratulate the Orange You Glad I Didn't Say Bandanas for their stellar performance and third-place finish!" The two tables of orange bandana players erupted in victory and swung their bandanas over their heads like a lasso. "For your efforts, you will each receive a forty-dollar gift card to the Double R Bar ranch's gift shop." The makeshift orange lassos increased speed, and the yelling went up a decibel.

"Thank you, thank you…job well done, Orange Ya Bandanas! We'll be waitin' in the gift shop for ya." The announcer placed the mic back in the stand and produced two team envelopes. "Now, I have in my hands the envelopes from the two teams that tied for first place! So, let's get right to it. The judging committee has decided we're gonna have a tiebreaker, and that tiebreaker will be pistol shootin'!"

The crowd cheered loudly.

"No, no, no...not at each other! We are going to take three members from each team around the corner to a gun range of sorts, and you'll each get six shots at a line of cans. The team with the highest score wins. Pretty simple and fair, right!?" Again, the crowd cheered loudly. "Okay," the announcer continued, "we need three shooters from each of these teams. The first team to play will be The Eight Banditos". The two tables of black bandanas jumped up from their table and began shooting fake bullets from their fingers into the air. "Immediately after the banditos, we will watch three members from The Princess, A Rock, and A Crown." The announcer shrugged his shoulders at the origin of the team name, and the crowd awaited some reaction from the tables to identify the players. The cheering dulled to a murmur when the tables remained seated.

Sarah's eyes grew wide as, from across the courtyard, she watched the sheriffs climb on top of their picnic table, screaming, "That's us! We won! We're gonna shoot guns!"

The other tables around them clapped politely and cupped their hands over their mouths, remarking to each other on the unfortunate position of having lost to such a maladjusted family.

Now fully aware of the circumstances, Sarah turned quickly and stared at Peter, who was sipping his beer. "That's our team name? What does that even mean? Never mind, because it doesn't matter…because I can't win…I'm the GM of the hotel!" Peter playfully lifted his eyes to look at Sarah and shrugged, refusing to lower his cup.

Steven quizzically looked at Peter. "Dude, what's with the

team name?"

Peter said simply, "You'd have to research your Hebrew names." As he replied, his hand held up his purple bandana and twirled it over his head. "We'd better get a move on. I think we are due at the range."

"All I can say is we're not going to win. I can't. It wouldn't look right." Sarah shook her head as the trio walked toward the range.

"It may not be up to you, Princess," retorted Peter.

"I have faith the sheriffs can't shoot straight," she calmly noted.

"Wasn't that a Don Knotts movie?" asked Steven.

"Yeah...funny. Tim Conway, too," confirmed Peter.

The crowd had gathered in a semi-circle around the ranch hands and announcer, who had placed six empty beer cans ten paces away down a dirt trail. The announcer raised his hand to show the audience his authentic Colt 45. Confident everyone had arrived, he addressed them again.

"As you can see, the men have placed a series of cans down the path a bit. I have in my hand here the gun that won the west. Six bullets, six cans. Three players from each team. Simple math...the team with the most cans hit wins."

"Wins what!" shouted Sheriff Tommy. Sarah shot him a look, and he quickly added, "Sir."

The announcer continued, "Well, I was getting' there. The players on the second-place team will each receive an all-day pass to…" he stared down at the card in his hand, "…Mr. Ringo's House of Western Wax. Come see the legends of the Old West in all their glory as Mr. Ringo leads a tour through the Tumbleweed Ghost Ranch. Fun for all ages!"

"That sounds like it stinks!" bellowed Sheriff Billy. He looked directly at Sarah and stated, "I ain't sayin' it."

In response, Sarah slowly raised her arm and made the sign of the cross over Billy's head.

Undaunted, the announcer plodded on, "As for the first-place prize, each member will receive a $100 gift certificate to…" his head again dipped to focus on his hand. When he lifted it, Sarah announced the location in unison with him. "…Saguaro's!"

Many in the crowd had heard of the restaurant and offered enthusiastic applause in recognition of a very worthwhile reward.

"Hey!" Steven exclaimed. "I know that place! That's where we had our date!" He immediately knew it was an overstatement but also wanted to gauge Sarah's reaction.

"Uh-huh," she replied, relenting to Steven's description. Then she threw in, "I haven't stopped thinking about it."

"Oh, c'mon," Steven pleaded sarcastically, "Throw me a bone,"

"Somehow, I don't think you are ever in need of a bone," chided Sarah.

"…er." supplied Peter on cue.

"Alright, Banditos, we need your three shooters to step up to the line to get instructions on handling your revolver from our trained tour guides," instructed the announcer.

The group of eight broke their huddle with a clap, and three young men in their early twenties turned on their heels and strode toward the firing line. One of three, a redhead with a scraggly beard and torn-off sleeves, stared intently at Sarah as he passed the purple team. As he approached, he stopped in front of Peter and turned toward him. Standing two feet from Peter, the Ginger let out a tribal scream, sending the sheriffs immediately to hug their father's leg, as Tom Sr. instinctively hugged his wife close to him, as he looked on in shock. Peter stood still and kept his gaze above the tormentor's head.

After an awkward silence, Peter said in a low growl, "Acting like an ass before we begin is your strategy? I hope when you grow up, you understand how to act properly around women and children."

The Ginger stepped backwards and spun to face his cohorts. As he walked away, Peter added, "Best of luck, son."

The three Banditos stood in front of the tour guide. "Okay, gents," the instructor said, " this is a loaded Colt 45 revolver. It holds six bullets, and there are six cans yonder."He pointed over his shoulder. "This here is the trigger. You point the business end of the gun toward the cans and pull it. Don't hold the gun the wrong way. God bless." He slapped the pistol into the hand of the first Bandito, then drew a line in the dirt with his boot heel.

The young man stood at the line and drew a sharp breath as he aimed the cans. The silence exploded with the release of the first bullet. When the first can flipped into the air and flew backwards, Sheriff Billy groped his father's leg even tighter, and Tom Sr. felt his son's pee stream down his calf. When the first Bandito had fired his last round, five of six cans had been hit, and Sherriff Tommy had released his father's leg and was now blubbering into his mother's lap.

Peter leaned toward Sarah and whispered, "I get the sense the sheriffs are officially off duty."

Sarah turned to take in the scene and immediately walked toward Tom Sr. Meanwhile, the second Bandito emptied his bullets in quick succession. Sarah could hear his teammates' congratulatory cheers and applause, which made her feel a bit better that the title was seemingly out of reach.

"Tom, are the boys okay?" she asked.

"Doesn't look like they take to gunfire."

Sarah bit her lower lip while taking in the circumstances. With another quick glance toward the parents, she dejectedly began, "Can you..."

"Looks like you, the Cap'n, and the sarcastic gentlemen will have to take on the challenge."

Sensing he had had enough, Sarah calmly placed her hand on Tom Sr.'s sleeve, and he drew a deep breath. She abruptly turned to view Peter and Steven assessing the situation, leaning against the fence, legs crossed, and thumbs in their belts.

Watching her approach, Steven spit his mythical tobacco juice on the dirt, pushed the brim of his hat upward, and studied her as she walked. "Problem, little lady?"

"No. No problem." Sarah walked past the impromptu cowhands toward the announcer. "Jim, what was the total for the Banditos?"

Jim raised the microphone to his mouth and announced, "Once again, Caballeros, the Banditos did some fine shootin' and came in with a combined score of 16 of 18 cans."

The remaining teams clapped again, and the Banditos let out another obnoxious roar.

Sarah met Peter and Steven at the shooting line. "We all know how this is going to go down. I fully expect you two testosterone-laden brain freezes to go twelve for twelve. That leaves me with the underwhelming task of missing three cans. I hope you like dressed-up mannequins."

As the three received their inadequate firearms training, Peter leaned toward Sarah and voiced his doubt, "So, you are going to purposely miss three cans?"

Sarah replied simply, "If I'm good enough to hit them, I can certainly miss them."

"I'm not questioning your skill…just your nature."

"I can't win my own event."

"But you can throw it."

"Exactly."

It took exactly ninety seconds, including reloading, for Steven and Peter to hand the revolver over to Sarah with a perfect score.

Peter moseyed back to the fence and leaned on the rails next to the Ginger, who remained quiet and still.

Sarah stepped to the line in the dirt and awkwardly lifted the revolver with both hands, struggling to keep it steady as she aimed toward the cans.

After several labored seconds that even had the ranch hands about to step in to help her, she pulled the trigger, and the only thing associated with the gun that didn't move were the cans. A puff of dust about two feet above the targets arose from the mound of dirt behind the cans.

Sarah let out an embarrassed giggle, and the Ginger let out a snort.

Sarah strained to raise the pistol once again and scrunched her face in determination to focus on the cans. She pulled the trigger once again, and immediately, a can flew into the air, tumbling end over end. The crowd cheered at first and then snickered a bit, when they realized Sarah had hit the fourth can in the sequence.

The Ginger exclaimed, "Lucky shot! We got this in the bag!" He fist-bumped his redneck friend beside him. Sarah's head went from side to side, releasing tension from her neck. Peter smirked.

The Ginger cocked his head toward Peter. "I'll be thinking about you when I'm enjoying my steak." He commented.

"$100 won't cover your bar tab." Peter stared into his eyes. "How 'bout I offer to double your winnings? Even if we tie."

"You're on! Easy money from my elders!" cackled the

Ginger. Peter held out his hand, and the Ginger grasped it to seal the bet just as four consecutive shots rang out. The Ginger looked at the range in time to see the last can hit the ground.

The crowd erupted in a guttural cheer. The announcer could only muster, "Wow, just wow. That's some fine shooting. By my count, that makes 17 out of 18 cans for The Princess, A Rock, and A Clown!"

"Crown," muttered Peter to himself.

The Ginger started to shout. "Hey! So you rigged…" Just then, he realized Peter was still grasping his hand, and the grip was tightening to the point where he knew it was best to stop his accusation. As he focused on Peter staring back at him, he confirmed it was the correct choice.

"Fair and square?" inquired Peter.

"Fair and square."

"It's good to know youngsters still respect their elders." Peter released his grip and stepped toward Sarah, who was speedily walking past.

"Don't." was all she offered as she made her way up the trail, still swinging the revolver in timing with her strides. Peter smiled broadly, as he watched her determined gait.

Steven appeared behind Peter's left ear. "You always did

know how to make a woman look sexy as she walked away from you."

"It's a gift, I suppose."

Neither broke their stare.

CHAPTER 24

The boys came over the hill toward the parking lot, taking significant draws from their refilled cups of beer. Many of the jeeps had left, including the red one that brought them to the ranch.

"She left us here!" exclaimed Steven. "You must have really pissed her off!"

Peter slowly moved his head from left to right, taking in the entire scene. When his focus reached the main house's front porch, he saw Sarah's unmistakable pair of boots rocking her chair back and forth agitatedly.

"No, she didn't," retorted Peter. "She's coming to terms."

Peter tapped Steven on the shoulder and finished his beer. Then, he began the 60-yard walk to the front porch. When they were within ten yards, the voice from the rocking chair questioned, "So, how did you know? Don't answer that. I don't want to know how you knew. How did you know?"

"Know what?" Questioned Peter. Sarah rocked the chair even harder.

Peter grinned and offered quickly, "You don't get to be the GM of a renowned resort property without being competitive."

"I didn't get there by beating my guests on company outings, either."

"Normally, I would agree with you. Competitiveness only gets you so far. You also have a good head for common sense."

"Then, how?"

"The ginger was the kicker."

"Ginger?"

"Not exactly the type of guest you mind embarrassing." Peter had reached the porch, but he decided to lean his shoulder against the side of the house, staying out of sight. "Besides, you knew the other guests were pulling for you to kick his ass."

Sarah's boots calmed the pace of the rocking chair.

"I let you influence my judgment. I made the wrong choice."

"If you meant that, you would have left with the other Jeeps."

Sarah's boots stopped the chair. Peter stood silent.

Steven announced his presence, "Anybody could have known you were going to kick the ginger's ass. He was a dick, and you don't like to lose."

A moment passed. The chair started to rock once again. Peter shot Steven a look to question his sanity. Steven shrugged.

"I really don't like being predictable." Sarah exhaled.

"Predictable or conforming?" Questioned Peter.

"There's a good choice between those two character flaws?"

"I mean conforming…as in being part of a group. Participating. Sharing."

"Giving in."

"Joining."

"You speak from self-diagnosis."

"I speak of one of my own faults, yes. I recognize it."

"You consider being in control of your own actions a fault?" Sarah questioned.

"Steadfast loyalty to any ideology blocks the ability to fully experience all that is being human.'

"Blocking things you can't control seems a worthy trait."

"At times."

"And at others?"

"Depriving. Starving. Suffocating."

"Suffocating?"

"Cutting off the basic things necessary to sustain our wellness."

"You have thought a great deal about this subject."

"I live it. I decry it."

"You sentenced it?" Sarah asked.

"I cloak myself in it."

"Yet, you are conforming with me right now."

"Yes."

"Why? Trying to make new habits?"

"Trying to help you break one."

"And?"

"It's exhausting."

"Good. We're even."

"Good. Can we leave now?"

"Yes. We can still make the game."

"The game? What game?"

"The All-Star game." Sarah stood from the rocking chair and waved her bandana toward the barn. The group watched as Jim, the announcer's, SUV kicked up dust as it approached the porch.

"Well, that was unpredictable."

Steven's feet remained planted as his head swiveled from the porch to the SUV, then back to the porch. "I don't have a fuckin' clue about what just happened."

CHAPTER 25

Steven entered the lobby, expecting to encounter another large group of strangers waiting impatiently for Sarah to escort them to the All-Star game at Chase Field. Instead, the lobby was relatively subdued, with a few stray business types awkwardly sporting brand-new caps that highlighted their everyman disconnect, while introducing themselves and waiting for their corporate sponsors to herd them toward whatever method of transportation would whisk them to the event.

As he walked across the expansive open space, his mood, which had already improved after a shower and change of clothing, continued to get better, as he realized this was a personal invitation from Sarah, not a resort function.

He couldn't control himself from smiling and giving two thumbs up when he caught Peter's eyes, as he spoke with Sarah. Her back was to Steven, and he turned downright giddy when he saw she was dressed in the same type of relaxed yet completely alluring attire she wore when they first met in that Irish bar in San Diego. Her guard was coming down.

Peter's attention shifted completely back to Sarah, and Steven caught her last few words as she told Peter about her abnormal passion for baseball.

"Then, you're talking to the wrong guy," Steven announced.

Sarah turned slightly to welcome him. "Don't tell me," she prodded, "you played baseball."

"All state."

"Impressive," Sarah offered quickly, leaning back a bit, inspecting Steven's build. "Let me guess. Second base. Batted sixth."

"Nice! Exactly." Steven was fascinated. "How'd you guess?"

"On the small side, decent batting average, good range, below average arm."

It was Peter's turn to smile uncontrollably. Steven's face went blank as he considered the accuracy of her impromptu evaluation. "All state," was all he could say in response.

"It really is quite impressive. I want to hear more about it. You can fill me in on our way over to BOB…sorry, Chase Field."

"BOB?" asked Steven.

"Bank One Ballpark," explained Peter. Gesturing toward

Sarah, he added, "Old habits die hard."

She placed her hand on his forearm. "It's ok, as long as we are aware of them."

"Indeed," Peter smirked at Steven as he turned to walk alongside Sarah toward the waiting driver of the resort's limo.

"Thank you for making the time to drive us to the park, David. Traffic must be a mess out there." Sarah reached up and gently squeezed the large man's shoulder. He bowed his head slightly in sincerity as he responded, "This is my pleasure, Ms. Garrity. Nothing I'd rather be doing."

"David, these are my guests, Mr. Max and Mr. Cross."

Steven reached his hand out first and shook David's hand. Pointing to himself and then Peter, he corrected, "Steven and Peter. We're friends with Ms. Garrity."

"Pleasure to meet you, David." Peter shook his hand. "This is a real treat. Thank you."

"Great to meet you both, as well. Let me know if you need anything at all," David replied. "Ms. Garrity, I spoke with our friend. He is indeed working the lot and has confirmed he is holding a nice place for us. He told me what to say as we approach the park."

"Thank you so much, David. You are one of a kind." Sarah pulled herself against David's right arm in a friendly embrace, and he gently nodded, accepting her compliment. "Let's get rolling. I want to make sure we see the intros. And, David, the latest TV contest winner, is singing the National Anthem."

David turned on his heels and led the three of them toward an impeccably clean yet subdued black limousine. He held the rear door and gestured for the two men to enter the large seating area.

Steven, who had positioned himself in front of Peter for a better view, immediately stopped and instructed David, "I wouldn't think of climbing in before our host." He and Peter turned to allow Sarah room to pass in front of them, only to spy her closing the front door from within.

Peter again could not hide his smile as he gestured for Steven to get into the car. "Looks like we're gonna have room to spread out." The two entered, and both faced the front of the vehicle.

Sarah peered back through the lowered partition and explained, "You'll find all sorts of goodies and beverages packed back there...vodka, bourbon, and beer if I remember correctly."

"Any conundrum?" Inquired Steven, displaying his memory skills.

Sarah raised her travel mug and grinned. "Thank you for remembering."

Peter poured two generous beverages and offered Steven his

glass. Steven begrudgingly snatched the drink from Peter's hand with a mock scowl. "Do you make a practice of sitting in the front of limos, ignoring your guests?" Steven inquired in an accusing tone.

"Oh!" Sarah glanced at David. "Maybe I should have been clearer. David isn't working tonight; he is coming with us. I wanted to keep him company on the way over to the game."

"Shit. Sorry, David. I guess I'm the ass."

"Again," Peter added. "You know, sometimes your mouth starts before your brain is finished thinking."

"Fuck you!" Steven waived his hand at Peter, playfully dismissing his remark. "Then you should let him call you Sarah, for Christ's sake."

"Oh, she's asked a thousand times," confessed David. "One time, I called her Sarah by mistake in front of visiting brass from corporate. She took it in stride. The brass, not so much. Right then and there, I decided it would always be Ms. Garrity. Eliminates the need for me to think."

"David and I have known each other for over twenty years. He's my rock and a very dear friend," Sarah confided.

Steven leaned forward, about to reply.

"That's OK. This will give us time to talk." Peter slapped his left hand on Steven's leg.

Steven lifted himself from his seat and moved along the side seating. He raised his glass to Peter and Sarah before taking an extended drag from its contents. Peter and Sarah followed in the same fashion.

The partition separating the front of the limo from the back began to close. Upon seeing Steven's mouth open in surprise and incredulity, Sarah could not help but let out a burst of laughter. She quickly lowered it back to its open state.

"Very good. Very good," congratulated Steven. "That would have sucked."

Sarah noticed Peter simply grinned and tipped his glass toward her to show his approval of her playful side. He also knew who he would sit next to during the game.

CHAPTER 26

It was even easier than he thought.

Peter simply pointed out things to David or asked him direct questions as the group walked toward their seats. Sarah's devotion to ensuring a smooth entry meant she would feel it necessary to lead the charge and arrive first at the seats in case something was awry. As for Steven, no effort would be needed to ensure he sat beside Sarah. He practically handcuffed himself to her. The only remaining question was the exact order.

When the group arrived at the correct section, Sarah spied an attendant and corralled him without missing a step. She had him walk with her as they drew closer to the seats, almost showing him to the numbered row on her tickets. She had asked for each back as soon as they entered the stadium, for just this scenario. The attendant dutifully nodded, as Sarah pointed to the four seats directly on the aisle. She shook his hand, slipped him a folded bill, and sent him on his way. As she raised her arm and gestured for her guests to enter, Steven bum rushed her with a polite, "These seats are fantastic!

Let's not hold anyone up in this crowd." His hands gripped her shoulders and turned her into the aisle. The seats were determined before she could react; an ambushed Sarah, a beaming Steven, a watchful David, and a contented Peter.

Sarah glanced down the row, assessing the alignment, and upon reaching Peter, she simply opened her hands in a "How did this happen?" gesture. Peter shrugged his shoulders with a bewildered look. At the same time, Steven shot Peter a "thumbs up" in front of his stomach while triumphantly pursing his lips. David studied Steven like a family's German Shepherd.

The four stood for a few moments to take in the view; upper deck, 5th row, directly beside third base, on the aisle. They collectively sat down, and Steven immediately turned toward Sarah, his back to David. Peter took that as his cue and started, "So, David, you're gay, right?"

David sat back in his seat and turned his face toward Peter. After initially contemplating the question, he answered, "No, I'm not. Did I say or do something to give you that impression?"

"Just a conclusion after noticing your deep feelings for Sarah, Ms. Garrity, are purely…chaste," explained Peter.

David turned toward Sarah and took note of Steven's positioning as he spoke with her. He turned back and nodded his head. "Unlike some."

"Most?"

"Most," David confirmed. He again turned to Sarah and waited momentarily for her "Get me out of this!" look. She did look, but in her "I've got this." way. That was the one he saw almost every time.

Satisfied, David relaxed and watched the groundskeepers prepare the field.

"Exes?" Peter interrogated.

This time, David stared straight ahead and grinned. "How many exes hang out together?"

Peter bought the group a beer from the passing vendor and passed them down the row. Each took a sip, except David, who placed the can beneath his feet.

"Related?" Peter persisted.

"Blood?"

"Yes."

"No."

"Step?"

"No."

"Adopted?"

"No."

"Ahhh, family friends?'

"Nope."

"You know, you and Sarah share the same conversation style. Are you sure you aren't related?"

David smiled again and turned to Peter with a slight laugh. "You know, she warned me more about your friend, but I believe I should watch my step with you, too."

Peter smiled. "Just makin' conversation."

Both men turned toward the field to see a national TV contest winner emerge from the dugout to sing the Star-spangled Banner. Just before the crowd got too loud and the announcer introduced her, Peter playfully offered, "Therapist?"

David shot Peter a sideways look with a smirk, then turned to enjoy the happenings on the field. The group respectfully stood and stayed silent during the National Anthem, and only Steven spoke as the players were announced. He informed Sarah of individual stats as each jogged from the dugout. Only once did Sarah comment, correcting the number of home runs for the American League first base starter. After that, no one spoke again until the players took the field for the top of the first inning.

When Steven resumed his position facing Sarah, David

gestured to Peter and went on the offensive. "After observing your friend's social skills, it is a pretty good guess the two of you aren't gay. So, why are you travelling together?"

Peter nodded his head slowly and replied, "Well, *he's* not gay. You're right about that."

He let the silence linger for a bit, then added, "High school friends. College friends. Work friends. Then, life intervened. This trip is a bit of a reset. It was time."

David stared at Steven, waiting for more. Nothing came. "OK. How long did life intervene?"

"Nine years."

"Time heals, huh?"

"Time smothers. Time shovels layers of apathy over emotional pain until you find a way to function again. Then, you move on." Peter looked at David and widened his eyes, daring him to ask for more.

David took the dare, "I can recommend a therapist."

Peter laughed, appreciating the humor. "It would be a full-time job. Unfortunately, it would also be very frustrating."

"How so?"

"I know the story. I know the facts. I know the ending. I've administered a healing solution."

"You certainly seem well-adjusted."

"So do you," said Peter, quickly. "But you know that's a farce."

"How do you know what I think of myself?" challenged David.

"It's what we all think of ourselves. It's when you think otherwise, you become an insufferable asshat."

David smiled widely, and the two clinked their plastic beer cups and toasted their imperfections.

From her detached location, Sarah spied on the male bonding and realized her seat position wasn't the result of an ambush by Steven, after all. It was Peter's plan all along.

The realization dawned on her so abruptly that she softly gasped and instinctively covered her mouth with her free hand. Oblivious to anything happening behind him, Steven was so encouraged by the response his conversation caused that he repeated his last phrase for extra effect. "No, no...I'm serious. I told the prospect, if you're going to buy from my competitor, put a little extra in the budget to buy yourself a shotgun, because you're going to want to blow your brains out every time you call them for service!"

Sarah sat back in her seat and chuckled a bit. Then, surprising even herself, she decided she wouldn't interfere with the seating arrangement. She would let Peter enjoy David's company, and Steven's effort would entertain her.

Sarah smiled at Steven and slapped her hand down on his, saying, "Don't tell me…he bought your equipment?!"

"He sure did. And many more since then. There was another time I…"

"Oh, look, Jones is up. Your hometown hero. I say he homers."

"He is great and treats the fans really well. Baltimore loves him. But I think he chases the low outside curveball for strike three too much."

"That is a very negative thought."

"Sorry. I just call it like it is. He chases too many outside curve balls."

"He also homers a lot."

"A shot says he strikes out."

"He can do anything else except strike out, and you will do a shot?"

"Yep. But, if he strikes out, you do the shot."

"You don't care about the odds, do you?"

"Not when I win, either way."

"OK, deal."

"Deal."

The two watched as the count went to three balls and two strikes.

Steven upped the ante as the pitcher accepted the throw from the catcher and went to the back of the mound. "Double?"

"I'd say the odds are much better for you now," countered Sarah.

"Sometimes you have to take a risk."

"Not when I don't win, either way."

"Afraid of not being in control?"

"Deal."

"Deal."

Steven believed he just cleared a major hurdle in bringing down Sarah's defenses.

Jones got the outside curve ball. But he watched it go by for ball four. As he jogged to first base, all Steven muttered was, "He never walks."

"It looked like he knew that pitch was coming," Sarah chided. "I'll wait here while you take your walk to the concession."

Steven stood to leave, but suddenly stopped and turned back to Sarah. "Don't let anyone take my seat." He waited for her confirmation.

"And miss the opportunity to win more wagers? Go on!! I'll even place my purse on your seat as dibs."

Steven again read that as progress. As he passed Peter on the way out of the aisle, he warned, "She put her purse on the seat to save it for me.'

"I saw that. Looks like you're on your way."

"Just a matter of time, my man. Just a matter of time."

When David overheard the remark, he withstood the urge to growl. It wasn't lost on Peter. As the two sat down, Peter assured David, "Sarah doesn't strike me as someone who would get picked up at a baseball game."

David let that sink in. He knew it was true.

Peter leaned forward and caught Sarah's eye. She smiled and waved her fingers toward him. He asked loud enough for her to hear, "Are you ok? Do you want David to switch seats? Get a breather?"

Sarah shook her head no and adamantly waved off the suggestion, saying, "Oh my, no! We are having a great time. I just won a bet! You two keep getting to know one another. It looks like you are getting along really well."

Peter replied, "We sure are. Why didn't you tell me David was a marine?"

"I keep that on the down low, in case I need him to demonstrate his skills to someone."

"Well, since he told me, he must think I'm a decent guy."

"Or he told you as a warning."

"Could be," Peter shot a glance at a grinning David, then back at Sarah. "No. I think it's because I am a decent guy."

"I won't even ask what you've been talking about."

"What or who?"

"Don't worry, Miss Garrity," David offered. "He's not breaking me down."

"I'm sure of that, David," stated Sarah, assuredly. "Mr. Max is no match for you."

As she spied Steven rushing down the stadium steps to get back to his seat, she sat back and confessed, in her mind, that she knew better than her last statement.

Steven shuffled past Peter and David, carrying two cups of whiskey, plopped himself down next to Sarah and immediately drank the entire contents of the first cup. He then challenged Sarah, stating, "I bought another for our next bet."

David turned to Peter and said simply, "I think you got as far in the last forty-five seconds as he will in nine innings. I feel better now."

Peter immediately questioned David, "You really think he could get that far in nine innings?"

Steven had made four trips to the concession area by the bottom of the sixth inning. With each successive pass, Peter and David found themselves steadying their companion as he maneuvered by them. Sarah had not lost any of the bets, and it was getting easier to set the odds, because Steven was drunkenly desperate to win at least one wager.

At the top of the seventh inning, Sarah excused herself, and as she exited the row, Steven yelled out to her, "Hey! Get another couple from the bar on your way back before they close down! I'm feeling lucky!"

Sarah grimaced, realizing she had enabled the situation. "I'll see what I can do."

Peter confirmed, "Nice work."

"I might have overestimated his limit," she confessed. "Now,

I'll have to deal with the consequences."

"Yes, you will."

As soon as Sarah climbed the steps toward the concourse, Peter tapped David's knee and pointed for him to take Sarah's seat. Sensing the situation called for such a move, David did not hesitate to do so. Peter then took David's empty seat, leaving an empty space at the end of the aisle. Of course, by the time Steven knew what happened, all he could mutter was a defeated, "Hey, I'm sitting here. I mean, you are sitting there. Not where you were. No room left for her." David's weighted hand on his shoulder quelled his one attempt at standing.

Sarah returned to the new seating arrangement and quietly took her seat at the end of the row, so as not to alert Steven, who was staring at second base for no apparent reason. "Is this some sort of idea to protect me?" she asked Peter.

"My idea to protect Steven."

"From me?"

"From himself."

Sarah leaned forward slightly and took another look at Steven, who was still staring at second base. "What is he watching?" she asked Peter.

"That is what we used to call zueling," he replied. Before she could ask, he continued, "Zueling is when your state of intoxication causes you to lose touch with your surroundings."

"Like daydreaming?"

"Yes, drunken daydreaming."

"How long will he stay like that?"

"No telling. But my guess is only a few more seconds. He is not completely drunk, just enough to be a bit confused. Soon, he will realize he is zueling and will self-correct as nonchalantly as he can."

"Zueling?"

"Zueling. It's a term we came up with for spacing out."

"Or daydreaming under the influence."

"DUI. I get it. You are pretty and witty, too."

"Did Mr. Max just say I was pretty?"

"Mr. Max isn't blind."

Sarah smiled and felt the blood rush to her cheeks. She returned the conversation to Steven's condition. "What happens then?"

"He will search for his beer, or what's left of his whiskey."

"Both of them are empty."

"Won't matter…it is the best attempt to look like he is still in control. He will quickly realize his mistake and stealthily hide the evidence."

"Then what happens?"

"He will sit quietly and watch the game. He will glance at the scoreboard to get all the pertinent information needed to make a relevant remark. Then, he will lean over and make it."

"What will you do?"

"WE...we will accept his comment graciously and allow him to continue the process."

"Process?"

"He will need another couple of minutes to align his mental and physical states. You know, make sure he can stand without falling forward and still make sense when he speaks."

"Will he be able to adjust?"

"Oh, sure. Like I said, he is not completely drunk. His brain got a little ahead of his body. Nothing a little recalibration can't fix. In five minutes, no one will know he was ever out of sorts."

When Peter finished speaking, he looked across the stadium and gently nudged Sarah to see what was coming. She turned her head to see the fans across the upper deck beginning "The Wave." Peter confirmed, "That should do the trick."

As the wave approached, it grew. It passed the section behind home plate and surged down the third baseline, until it was upon them. As everyone in front and behind them stood, yelled, and waved their arms high into the sky, the four of them remained seated. But it was only Steven who had done so, due to zueling. Both Sarah and Peter took note that neither had moved. Before they could compare their reasons for staying seated, Sarah nudged Peter and nodded toward Steven, who had pulled himself back to reality and was raising his empty cup to his lips. When he realized it was empty, he slowly placed the container on the pavement under his seat and peered at the center field scoreboard, without taking in any of its offered information.

The wave came around home plate again, and Peter and Sarah looked at one another as it passed, while Steven steadied himself on David's shoulder, to stand and wave his opposite arm skyward. Upon taking his seat, Steven leaned over David and cajoled, "What's wrong?! Are you two too tired to stand up? Let's have a little fun! Loosen up!" Steven turned quickly to David and exclaimed, "David, tell these two to loosen up!"

"Loosen up, you two," David offered in jest. He noticed Sarah's face and smile, as she was caught up in the moment and, without thought, held onto Peter's forearm, as she leaned into him gleefully. He had not witnessed that particular expression in many years. Genuine enjoyment.

David's glance moved to Peter, who immediately translated his expression into a confirmation of what was happening. It jolted Peter. How had he not noticed the impromptu embrace? He withstood his first instinct to pull away from Sarah's grasp. He knew that would just be rude and weird. But this was foreign to him, and so far out of character, he couldn't understand how he got into this position. The best he could muster was a smirk to David that suggested, "Cut it out. There is nothing to see here."

David simply raised his eyebrows to suggest, "Yeah, right."

It was enough to diffuse the moment, while Peter worked on correcting the situation. It was, after all, just a friendly gesture. Peter refused to overanalyze it. Attraction to Sarah Garrity was not going to happen.

CHAPTER 27

After the game, won by the American League 5-2, the foursome lingered and allowed the crowd to work its way to the exits. True to form, Steven had rebounded well enough to be socially interactive, even enough to realize his mission of connecting with Sarah would be aborted, at least temporarily. In fact, as the four leaned against some empty seats in an abandoned aisle, it was in those several minutes that the best conversation was enjoyed. By the time they made their way to street level and exited to relatively small huddles of neon-lit humanity, everyone in their group was laughing.

"Where to next?" Steven requested. The laughter died quickly as the group stood in the colored light. At that moment, it was clear no one had anticipated additional plans after the game.

After several moments, Peter shrugged his shoulders and offered, "I am a bit hungry."

Sarah shrugged back and added, "I could eat."

"Yeah! It's agreed, then. There must be something nearby." Steven led the way. "Let's go this way." He started walking quickly, gesturing for the others to follow.

"Perhaps, I should get the car and wait for you to..." began David, readily accepting that he was still the driver and Sarah's employee.

"Nonsense!" she cut him off. Sarah placed her arm inside David's, adding, "You're not leaving my side."

"Our side." Peter placed his arm inside David's other arm.

"C'mon, you guys! I'm starving!" shouted Steven, waving his arms from nearly a block away.

"He moves pretty fast," deadpanned David.

"In more ways than one." The group of three walked in unison toward Steven.

"I see what you did there," said Peter. "On point."

After approximately fifteen yards, the three of them realized it was hard to walk in unison, and laughing only made them slower. David kept his eyes focused on Steven because he had kept walking, and they were not gaining any ground. He watched as Steven abruptly stopped and looked up, opened a large wooden door, peered inside, then leaned back and gave a thumbs-up, before disappearing inside.

The group approached the location a minute later, and Peter motioned before David could alert them that this was where Steven chose. "What was he looking at?" Asked Sarah. David wondered why he ever doubted they both would be aware of their surroundings, even when genuinely engaged in conversation.

The three raised their heads and read the bar's name – Throwbacks. Below the commercial signage was a hand-written message taped to the window that simply read, "In here, we throw back shots, food, pictures & tunes."

David pulled the door handle and surveyed inside. Satisfied, he repositioned his body behind the open door and motioned Sarah to enter.

Sarah responded with a sarcastic smile and commented, "Into the lion's den," as she passed. When all three were inside, trepidation was replaced by relief. Peter immediately took in the large but manageable crowd and was impressed that the demographics ranged from mid-twenties to mid-sixties, including a good mix of genders. The song playing as they entered was Van Morrison's "Caravan," and both young and old were appreciating the Irish master's rhythm and lyrics.

Several groups swayed and sang along on the parquet dance floor positioned in the middle of the bar with tabled seating on all sides. It was obvious from the invisible fence protecting it that, if you were on the dance floor, you were dancing, or at least swaying. There was to be no standing while on the parquet.

The bar was along the wall with ample stools. Its worn mahogany finish stretched nearly sixty feet. The business side was well attended by three attentive bartenders who matched the bar's demographics: two women, one mid-twenties, the other mid-forties, and one weathered hipster dude, who allowed the ladies to run the show, while he supplied clean glasses and shot elixirs, while working the register. Behind the bar, in typical fashion, a mirror reflected the clientele clamoring to be noticed, while simultaneously helping to illuminate the bottles of over-priced liquor. It quickly became obvious this was the weathered dude's chemistry set, by the way his hands knew where to grab without any need to look.

At the end of the bar stood a refurbished Wurlitzer jukebox, which was clearly the heart and soul of the establishment. Even Peter wondered what jewels were stashed in its collection of throwback classics. Sarah, David, and Peter all saw Steven's hand waving them toward his position next to the bright colored lights of the Wurlitzer. They all checked each other for approval before David led the charge through the thick but accommodating crowd.

Peter could only think it was Van's music that made them so malleable. He considered what might happen to the mood of the masses if AC/DC played next. Fortunately, the group of three arrived near Steven, but too many people still surrounded them to make it comfortable. Steven pointed each of the three to positions behind others seated at the bar. When he was satisfied, he leaned over the edge of the bar and announced, "OK, up you go!" and lifted his arms to highlight his command. The four youngsters seated in front of Peter, Sarah, David, and Steven rose in unison and relinquished their seats. As they slid by, they smiled and welcomed the usurpers with "Hi," "Welcome," and "Enjoy." As Steven's seat became available, he exchanged a fist pump and man-hug with the happy lad, who moved aside.

"Thanks again, Steven."

"No worries, Jason. My pleasure. Thank you."

Steven patted the young man on the back as he turned into his newly acquired seat. Once positioned, he checked on his three companions with a broad, toothy smile and asked, "What'll you have?"

"How much?" Inquired Peter.

"I asked nicely."

"How much?" Repeated Sarah.

"I paid their check. They've been here since the start of the game," explained Steven.

After a brief pause, David repeated, "How much?"

Steven feigned an insulted look and questioned, "What do you mean? I told you. I paid their check. No small amount, I'll have you know!"

The three now stared at Steven.

"I paid their check," Steven repeated, motioning for the weathered bartender to come visit.

Peter watched the bartender approach and accuse Steven. "No way you wave him down when there are two women behind the bar, unless you wanted to change the subject! How much?!" All three stares were on Steven again.

After a heavy sigh, Steven admitted, "I paid their bill....and gave them each a Franklin."

"A Franklin?!" Sarah couldn't help but laugh. "A Franklin? They must have known you were a cool dude! They might have moved for a Jackson! Or maybe even a Hamilton and a Lincoln!" She cupped her hands to her mouth, after an inadvertent snort of laughter, which only made her laugh harder.

Peter laughed with her, thoroughly enjoying her antics at Steven's expense. The bartender arrived and placed both hands on the bar, surveying his customers. Deciding the uncontrolled laughing from the first two would continue for a while longer, he turned to David, who was preoccupied with observing Sarah and

Peter, then settled on Steven, who sat quietly at the end of the bar, red-faced.

"Yes, sir?"

Steven looked straight into the mirror and replied, "Three Stella's and a Diet Coke."

The weathered bartender turned to face the mirror and addressed Steven's reflection, while motioning at the lineup of beers on the shelf. "Stella's not throwback."

Steven immediately responded, "Three Miller Hi Life's and a Tab."

"There you go," said the weathered bartender, as he bent into the refrigerator in front of him. "Any eats?"

"Do you have Calamari?" Asked Steven.

"Is Calamari throwback?"

Steven pursed his lips in frustration, and his hand curled into a fist. "Two orders of mozzarella sticks and an order of nachos," interjected Peter, recovering from his impromptu interlude.

"Oooh, and onion rings!" added Sarah.

"There you go," congratulated the bartender as he retreated into the middle of the bar to work the register.

"Glad to see you two are ok. Thought I was gonna have to

sedate you," said Steven.

"Oh, wow," Sarah chuckled. "I haven't laughed like that in a long time! I don't think I've snorted since college."

"Well, I was embarrassed for you," lamented Steven.

"C'mon Steven, it was funny!" offered Sarah, still giggling as she smiled at him. "Besides, I know you aren't that thin-skinned to be upset with me."

"You seem to have me all figured out, huh?" Challenged Steven, sensing things were focusing on him again.

Sarah, Peter, and David all responded at once, "Uh-huh," causing them to begin laughing again. Sarah's hand reached for Peter's forearm, and she grabbed his sleeve. David watched Peter look at her hand and, after a few moments, remove his arm to look at his phone.

They devoured their plates of food, and only a puddle of hardening Cheez-Whiz was left of the nachos and the group had settled into contentment as they sipped on their drinks, while enjoying song after song of decades-old music that perfectly set the tone for conversation without being overbearing.

Steven waited patiently in his seat and listened for the songs he had programmed into the jukebox, before the others arrived. When he heard the opening to "Get Down Tonight" by KC and the

Sunshine Band, he stood from his seat and poked his face between Peter and Sarah.

"You can't hear this song and not want to dance!" stated Steven, placing his open hand over Sarah's shoulder.

The move surprised everyone, including Sarah. At first, she listened to be sure of the song, then glanced at David with a look that said, "How did this happen? I'm ok, but how in the hell did this happen?"

David shifted in his seat and grunted, disappointed he let his guard down but resisted the impulse to interfere. This wasn't exactly an overly aggressive move on Steven's part, and Sarah was certainly not in danger.

The way Peter reacted surprised him, too. He stood and before Steven could object, took Sarah by the hand and said, "Now that you mention it, I do feel like dancing. Ms. Garrity, will you do me the pleasure?" Even more confused, Sarah walked toward the parquet to dance with Peter, leaving Steven slumped against the bar.

Evidently, the song represented a cue for many patrons as they shuffled off the dance floor, clearing ample space for the entering couple.

Once established, Sarah and Peter turned to each other and found the beat. Sarah followed Peter's lead and mimicked his swaying and slight arm-flailing style. It was ok, she thought. At least he had a bit of rhythm.

"You're not bad," she assured Peter.

"That is a predictable woman's comment to a guy trying not to look foolish on the dance floor. And, if I remember correctly, you don't like to be predictable."

Sarah accepted she was caught and answered, "Ok, then. What you are doing is passable, maybe even decent."

"Exactly."

"Exactly, what?"

"That is exactly what I was aiming for,"

"Passable?"

"Unmemorable."

"Does that mean you have more moves than this?"

"Sure. Every guy always has at least two dance styles."

"Which is this one?" Sarah smiled back quizzically.

"This one? Doing a friend a favor."

"Favor?"

"You'd rather be out here with Steven?"

"I could have said no."

"You could have, but you wouldn't have. That would have been a buzz kill. And it would have been your fault. Pretty well-played by Steven, actually."

"Do you two ever stop competing?"

"I already told you a couple days ago, I'm not playing."

"What are you doing, then?"

"Obstructing."

Sarah looked into Peter's eyes and asked, "Why?"

The question caught Peter off guard. His immediate thought of a response startled him. In doing so, he temporarily lost his rhythm and stopped dancing. Sarah was still locked onto his eyes.

Peter chose his second answer. "I guess I am playing. But my goal is to win by getting in his way."

"Why did you have to think about your answer?"

"I'm a little embarrassed. I didn't know I was playing." In reality, Peter was startled to acknowledge his actions were motivated by his attraction to Sarah Garrity.

The couple danced again.

"What's the other dance?" Sarah requested.

"The real deal."

"Which means?"

"Good, bad, or ugly, the guy's best moves are on display for all to see."

"Ohhh, I've seen that!" Sarah exclaimed.

"I'm sure you have. Usually happens at wedding receptions, after the third hour."

"Why don't guys just choose that one all the time?"

"Kinda like watching romantic comedies. Not our gig unless we are drunk. Plus, it's risky."

"Risky? Why?"

"Most guys have no idea what their real deal dance actually looks like. It doesn't matter to them. But, if it's ugly, it can flatten a relationship and repulse every other female in sight."

Sarah smiled again. "You think women care?"

"Once it's on display, it can define you. I've witnessed women point and whisper, as soon as unfortunate dancers enter a room. Yeah, it's risky."

"And if the woman is ok with the real deal? What happens then?"

"Major hurdle passed. Major. The guy knows he is free and clear, and the woman's friends have no choice but to accept his dancing, too."

"Really?"

"It's science."

Sarah watched Peter continue his "do a friend a favor dance" for a few more seconds, then blurted out, "Let me see it!"

Peter knew what she meant and shook his index finger at her. "You aren't ready."

"Let me see it!" Sarah demanded. Then, she slyly added, "What's the risk?"

Again, Peter realized there was no good immediate answer, and for a second time, he stopped dancing. He listened closely to the song and estimated when there were twenty seconds left.

Without notice, his entire body began moving, and his limbs moved at varying angles. His hands rose above his waist and punctuated the beat and change in notes. He reached for Sarah's hand and pulled her closer, placing his opposite hand gently around her waist. Together, they swayed deliberately to the song, as the music trailed off.

They stood facing each other and locked eyes. Neither looked away. Sarah confirmed, "You really are a good dancer. I'm not repulsed."

Peter turned on his heel and maintained his grasp on her

hand, while they exited the dance floor. "Never had a complaint," he replied in a purposely chauvinistic style. From across the room, he noticed a twenty-something guy giving him a thumbs-up. Peter grinned. He couldn't help it, and for the first time in a long time, he didn't suppress it.

Upon returning to the bar, David raised his eyebrows as Peter approached, and two fresh beers were waiting for them. The seat beside Sarah had opened, and Steven sat waiting for her return.

"Well, I suppose you lost your interest in dancing with me after suffering through that," Steven said sympathetically.

"Let a girl quench her thirst," replied Sarah, reaching for her beer and taking her seat between the two friends.

"When was the last time you danced in a bar?" Questioned David.

Sarah shot him a playful look. "*Et tu*, Da-veed?! You are supposed to watch my back!"

"Just curious. Looked like you were having fun," defended David, shrugging his shoulders while sipping on his Tab.

Peter sat back on his bar stool, allowing the two to clearly stare at each other.

Sarah dropped her jaw and addressed David. "Whatever. I'm allowed to have fun. So are you, you know."

"Absolutely. I enjoyed watching you have fun, that's all," David replied.

"I dance in bars all the time. It's a hobby of mine," Sarah challenged.

Peter couldn't help but smile as the two confidants verbally sparred. Certainly, this was an out-of-the-ordinary experience for them.

"Must happen when I'm not around," answered David.

"You aren't invited everywhere I go," shot back Sarah.

"Evidently. So, tell me…."

Peter sat forward to insert himself between their stares. "Why would two people who care about each other so much quarrel about having fun?"

Sarah and David immediately realized the path they were on and abruptly changed their attitudes.

"Because I'm a jerk," offered David.

"And I have to be in control," confessed Sarah apologetically.

Both Sarah and David reached for each other's hands in front of Peter to shake and end the conversation.

"So, does that mean you'll dance with me?" Petitioned Steven.

"Yes, Steven. I owe you a dance," Sarah concluded.

"Great. Stairway to Heaven just came on. Let's go." Steven put out his hand, and Sarah obliged.

"Should have listened for the song before answering." Cajoled Peter, as the two walked toward the dance floor.

Peter and David continued to watch as they joined together for the slow part of the classic song. Both expressed surprise when Steven's hand stayed high around Sarah's waist.

"Is she taming him?" Questioned David.

"Good question. She's definitely done something to him. Being a gentleman goes against his instincts."

"Think it's part of a bigger plan?" Searched David.

"It's big, alright. He's respecting her," concluded Peter. Both men drank their beverages.

"Now I really have to keep an eye on him," David remarked.

"Not him. Her," corrected Peter.

"Aye. Her," David acknowledged.

The two of them sat and watched silently, searching for contradictory evidence to their summation, but receiving confirmation instead.

"We went to the same high school," stated David directly.

"Classmates?" Peter considered the statement for a moment.

"Ok, classmates. But there is more to it, correct?"

"Not classmates. I was two years behind her. We went to a large public school together. I knew her…of her. No surprise there. She didn't know me."

Peter remained silent.

"She didn't know me, but she was nice to me…naturally nice. I was big for my age, so I was a target for the upperclassmen. She kept the junior and senior jocks from picking on me. Typical teenage stuff, I guess. They only picked on me a few times, trying to start something with the biggest little kid. Every time, she would step in and make them feel stupid for picking on underclassmen. She had a way about her…"

"Had?" Peter questioned.

"Has…and always had," David corrected himself. "Sarah always had a way of imposing her will on those guys. She was always smarter than all of them. And every time she saved me from a group beating, and they would walk away, she'd turn her head and shoot me a smile, as if to say, 'I've got your back.' That smile almost made me look forward to the next time the jocks would come around looking for a fight."

David stopped there for effect. After a few moments, he made his point. "That is why I will always have her back."

"I can tell you are a good friend to her, David. And I can also tell she's a good friend to you," Peter respectfully stated.

"Yes."

"But there is still more than that. What you just described is a high school crush on the prettiest, most popular girl in school. It didn't hurt she was two years older than you, either."

"So?"

"So, why is there no sense of a crush in your relationship? Not even a remnant. I mean the scenarios are these: One: you asked her out, and she said no. Very unlikely you would remain close for so long. Two: you asked her out, and she said yes. In which case, the two of you still defy the odds because there had to be a breakup in there somewhere. Again, no remnant of a crush remains. I know what you felt for Sarah was not platonic. The question is how she felt about you. That would clear things up a bit."

David's face became stern, in part because he wasn't in control of the conversation any longer. "Three: I never asked her out, or four: she asked me out, and I said no."

Peter motioned at the surly but competent bartender for another round.

"Nope. Neither works without leaving a remnant," dismissed Peter, disregarding the noticeable change in David's demeanor.

"Will you stop saying remnant?" confronted David. "It's starting to bug me. Pick a new word."

Peter swigged his beer and offered, "Residue?"

"Stick with remnant.'

Peter let David off the hook, sensing the bar was not the place to press for more information. "Oh, look…it's gotten to the fast part of Stairway to Heaven, and Steven doesn't know what to do."

David refocused and laughed, "Rookie mistake. He's just swinging his hips faster."

Steven and Sarah turned with the music, and Sarah shot the two men at the bar an amused, but patient, look of bewilderment.

"There is more," confided David.

Peter again chose to remain silent but turned his ear toward David.

"Near the end of her senior year, there was a field party. A big one. Blowout. Two of my friends and I heard about it and crashed it. We were able to score a case of beer and a bottle from a guy outside the liquor store, and we hung by ourselves on the outskirts of the main party. We knew our place. We were only sophomores, but I was bigger…and stronger. It was cool to hear the music and laughter and see the glow of the bonfire. It was a clear night with a ton of stars. As we got drunk, we'd stare up at them and laugh at how they were getting blurry. We kept to ourselves, though…at least until the beer and bottle were both finished." David paused. Peter didn't say a word, and he continued.

"It didn't take much for us to get our courage up. We were already buzzed. We decided to make our way into the party and bum some beer from the keg. Well, no sooner had we picked up the red cups than I get grabbed from behind and put into a full Nelson."

"A jock?" Peter concluded.

"A drunken jock. More drunk than me. With three other drunken jocks," specified David. "I was able to shed the one who had me in the full Nelson, and I started to plead my case, when I got cold-cocked by one of his buddies. I stumbled but didn't go down. I should have gone down. Because the next thing I remember was waking up in the hospital. They kept me for a few days. Doctor told me I was hit on the head by something hard, probably a bottle that didn't break."

At this point, Peter knew two things. First, Stairway to Heaven was ending, and second, David was going to have to make his point.

"Anyway, when my buddies came by to visit, I thanked them for getting me to the hospital. Turns out, it wasn't them. It was…"

"Sarah Garrity," finished Peter.

"Yes."

303

"Only adds to your crush, no?" interrogated Peter.

"Well, you would think so. And it did. Until I returned to school and found out the jock that hit me with, in fact, a full bottle of vodka was expelled from school a week before graduation. And that jock was Sarah's boyfriend."

Here it comes, thought Peter.

"I wanted to repay her kindness, so I went to the school administration and convinced them to let the guy graduate with his class and thereby keep his college scholarship."

"And...?"

"And everything was fine. When she learned what I did, she sought me out and thanked me. She told me she broke up with him the day after the party, but was happy he would keep his scholarship. She graduated. I fell all over myself, trying to ask her out. Before I could even make a complete sentence, she figured it out and enthusiastically told me she was going to the West Coast to work at a restaurant all summer, before leaving for college. In those days, there were no cell phones, no email, and long-distance charges, so I knew that was her way of telling me, 'Have a nice life.' Everything was fine. Fine. Fucking fine. I became the upperclassman jock who looked for the biggest little kid. I got drunk a lot. I got high a lot. I fought with my parents. I didn't date anyone, except when I wanted to score or get a prom date. The only time I ran into Sarah when she came back from college for Christmas break. I was too wasted to hold a conversation. By the time graduation came around, I was the asshole I swore I'd never be. The worst part was I didn't know it, or rather, I accepted it. Finally, my father intervened and convinced me to enlist in the Marines. Well, it was really an ultimatum…join the service, or get the fuck out. Turns out, I was good at being a marine. I loved the discipline. But I never could let go of the asshole, so when my superiors told me that despite my stellar service, I would never move beyond my current rank due to my anger issues, I accepted their feedback and took my leave. Seems that didn't help my attitude. I went from bar to bar, being a bouncer and getting into fights, looking for fights, getting drunk, and getting high. One night, years after I last saw her, Sarah 'happens' into one of the dives I worked in. She tells me she was wondering if I might want a more reserved career. I tell her to get the hell out of the bar. I didn't need or want her fucking charity."

When Robert Plant elongated the song's final line, David summed up his story. "Three weeks later, I tracked her down to the resort and offered to do anything she needed. She offered me this position…after going through rehab. And here I am today."

David held up his soft drink as evidence of his sobriety.

"Crush was gone?" Peter pondered.

"Obliterated."

"Okay."

"I'm not good enough for her. Guilt and embarrassment can cripple a man."

That statement hit home with unexpected precision. Again, Peter stated, "Okay." This time, he meant it.

"Well, well, well…I suppose we know who Sarah prefers as a dance partner," boasted Steven, returning to the bar with Sarah.

"Congratulations. I've had enough fun tonight. I'm heading back to the hotel." Peter abruptly stood, which took Sarah and Steven by surprise. David studied Peter's sudden change in demeanor.

"No! Wait. What?" Steven exclaimed.

"Really?" quizzed Sarah.

Peter chose to look at Sarah when he responded. "Yes. It's OK. I've had a good time. Thank you. I've had my fill, that's all. Please, the three of you should continue. I'll get a ride back."

"Can't have that," David plainly spoke. "I'll run you back, then come back for Sarah and Steven.

"Perf-" began Steven.

"That's fine. Let's go," responded Peter.

Sarah wasn't sure what was happening, but she made an

immediate decision. "Nonsense! We don't split up! If you go, we all go."

"That isn't what I meant to do. You seem like you want to stay. Stay," instructed Peter.

"It is fun…together. You are right. The best decision is to sacrifice an hour of fun for an hour of sleep. I've got an early morning," stated Sarah, reaching for her purse.

"What's happening?!" Steven implored.

"Stay or go. That's fine. I need some air. I'll walk back. David, thanks for the talk and the ride," stated Peter flatly. "Good night, everyone." He began walking toward the door.

"Peter. Peter, it's two miles back to the resort. Don't walk by yourself," Sarah started toward the door, then turned her head back toward David and demanded, "What happened?" She then continued toward the exit.

As she left, David and Steven looked at each other and shouted nearly the same thing.

"Wait up! I'm not letting you walk back without me!" shouted David.

"Wait up! I'm not letting you walk back with him!" shouted Steven.

Both men followed Sarah and Peter through the door. By the

time they reached the street, Sarah had caught up with Peter and walked alongside him. Steven quickened his stride when David grabbed his arm. "Let her have her space. Give her a few minutes."

"How do you know she wants space?" Questioned Steven.

"Her walk and her body language. She wants answers," responded David.

Sarah and Peter walked for a few hundred yards without saying a word. Every ten yards, she would turn her head and stare at him, as he kept his gaze straight ahead.

She turned her head one last time, and Peter broke the silence. "I have very good peripheral vision."

"Could have fooled me."

"I apologize for the sudden departure back there. It was rude," lamented Peter.

"Not so much rude as...concerning?" Sarah questioned her own choice of words.

"Disconcerting," offered Peter.

"Strange."

"Weird."

"One of those."

Peter turned his head toward Sarah and briefly smiled.

"Maybe all of those."

Sarah smiled back. "Well…look how far we've come in less than a week. We've let our guards down a bit."

"Could be that. Or it could be the darker parts couldn't be subdued anymore. I suppose they had to show up some time to be counted," Peter confided.

"Oh, c'mon!" Sarah latched onto Peter's arm as they walked. "Darker parts? You had a moment. We all do." She shook his arm slightly and smiled up at him.

Peter gently pulled his arm away from Sarah. In the short distance behind them, Steven couldn't help but break into a hopeful smile. David cocked his head and focused on the couple ahead.

Peter stopped and turned toward Sarah. She stopped as well and looked into his eyes. She realized his stare was much more intense than when they were on the dance floor.

"You like to fix people. I don't want to be fixed," surmised Peter.

"Fix?" Sarah took a slight step backward. "How did you get there?"

"Look. I don't want to…"

"You don't want to what? You don't want to blame whatever happened back there on me?"

"I don't…didn't want to draw any attention or concern. I just wanted to go," Peter explained.

"Didn't want to draw attention?" Sarah sarcastically questioned. "And I'm sorry, you get my concern, too!" She grabbed his arm again and pulled it toward her. "What is this wall you put up? Do you always need to be in control? Is anyone allowed?"

"Allowed?"

"Near you." Sarah stared into Peter's eyes, and his eyes pierced hers.

"Stop," Peter stated firmly. "No one is allowed close enough to judge me. I won't give them a reason to judge me."

"Peter," Sarah said softly. "I don't know you. I only know what you've shown me…the same as everyone else in your life."

Peter drew in a sharp breath. "That's best."

"Is that the way you want it?" Sarah examined.

Peter's attention unlocked from Sarah's and focused on Steven and David, as they covered the last few yards toward them. His eyes lingered on Steven for a long moment.

"Exactly how I want it."

As Peter turned to leave, Sarah's grasp on his arm released, and her hands went instinctively to the chain around her neck. Her expression changed from concern for Peter to concern for herself as her fingers searched her neckline for the cross that always hung there. She reached inside her partially unbuttoned shirt in search of its necklace chain. It took her a couple of frantic seconds to confirm it was no longer there.

"Oh no! Oh no! Please, no!" Sarah involuntarily sounded. Steven immediately answered, "What? What happened!" But David knew.

Peter stopped in his tracks and realized from her tone Sarah's distress had nothing to do with him. He turned back to see Sarah clutching at her neck, while searching the cobblestones surrounding her. Instantaneously, the four of their heads swept the ground, looking for whatever it was that caused Sarah's reaction.

Steven nudged David and asked quietly, "What are we looking for?"

David whispered, "Her cross."

The four returned to their search, circling the area in odd, disordered patterns. After several moments, David stood up straight and loudly said, "Steven! What are you doing? She never even went that far." Steven came back inside the correct boundaries. David continued, "Let's use this slight break to collect ourselves and develop a better game plan."

"Good idea," responded Steven. "What does it look like?"

"I remember it," said Peter. "It's silver, not very large or ornate. It slightly beveled around its edges. Hardly noticeable."

"Was it expensive?" Requested Steven.

"No." Sarah plainly replied, her voice quivering. "Maybe. I don't know. It was my grandmother's. She gave it to me when I was eighteen. Its worth is in her gift." Sarah lifted her head to reveal tears on her cheeks.

"Everyone come to me. We will start here four-across and go back toward the bar." David directed. "If we don't find it between here and there, we'll go back to the stadium."

"It's between here and the bar," Peter confirmed. "It was still on when we were on the dance floor."

"Are you sure?" questioned David.

"I wouldn't have said anything if I wasn't."

David moved on. "Steven?"

Steven lifted his head. "What?"

"Do you recall if Sarah was wearing the necklace when you danced?"

Steven opened his mouth but paused before speaking. Finally, he admitted, "I don't know."

"Ok," accepted David. "It doesn't matter. We know it is between here and the dance floor. We will walk together, slowly and deliberately, back to the bar. Everyone has a four-foot area to cover."

The three men began to recreate their path, but Sarah stood still. They stopped and turned back toward her, each with a quizzical look. She lifted her phone toward her ear.

"I'm calling the bar," she explained. "If they say they don't have it. I'll go back tomorrow and ask again."

"What about the street?" Implored Steven.

"We've walked over a mile. The chances of us finding it are almost zero. I can't have you spending hours looking for a necklace," stated Sarah.

"We should try," Steven replied. "It's important to you."

Sarah smiled gratefully. "It is important to me. Thank you. But it's...Hello? Hi, I'm sorry to call, but I believe I may have lost my necklace in the bar. We were seated at the bar and danced a bit. Has anyone turned it in?" She listened for a few seconds. "Yes, that's us. It is a silver cross with a silver chain." A few more seconds passed. "That is fine. My name is Sarah Garrity. Yes, that is my cell number, and I'll be sure to have it on me. Thank you for looking. I'll wait for your call." Sarah clicked the end button and then smiled at her company. All three awkwardly smiled back.

"That was the bartender. He said he remembered us and would check the bar area and dance floor and call me back if he found it."

Steven beat David to the response. "What if he doesn't find it?"

"It doesn't matter," Sarah responded. She smiled again. This time, Peter's smile was natural and bold. He wasn't sure why he smiled so confidently, but he saw Sarah's certainty and peace in hers.

Sarah continued, "My grandmother gave me that cross when I was eighteen. I've worn it ever since. I just now realized that what she told me when she gave it to me has come true. And my heart is happy!"

Steven again took the lead. "What did she tell you that would completely change your outlook about losing it?"

Sarah was prepared to answer quickly. "When she placed it in my hand, she placed her hand over it and said, 'Keep this with you and wear it for strength. Draw from it and give your problems to it. It will be with you on all days, the best ones and the worst. But there will be a day when it will reveal how much you are loved. On that day, you'll realize its true meaning. Your worries and fears will no longer have a hold on you, and the cross you used as an anchor, a ladder, and a crutch will be at the center of an act of unity and thoughtless love. Until then, travel your life together and use it as you need.'" When she finished, Sarah's cheeks were again lined with tears, but her face was radiant with joy.

They stood silently. Sarah offered clarity. "I always remembered what she said to me. But the part I remembered most clearly was the term 'thoughtless love'. I know that is what she said because when she said it, I thought, 'What a strange phrase?' I mean, most everyone would say "unconditional love" or "selfless love", and if she had said it that way, it may never have stuck with me. My grandmother said, 'thoughtless love'. As the years passed, I never believed I'd witness it. It never made the slightest bit of sense. I mean, how could it? What is the definition of thoughtless love?"

Sarah lifted her arms and pointed at the three men in front of her. "The three of you just gave me the gift of thoughtless love. For the last several minutes, and who knows for how much longer, each of you was prepared to look for a lost necklace, in terrible lighting, along a mile-long stretch of cobblestoned path…without giving it a thought."

The three men threw their shoulders back. Her message hit them directly, and they understood the part they had played. Steven was noticeably surprised and thrilled.

Sarah turned her eyes toward the sky and simply said,

"Thanks, Mom-Mom. Thank you, Jesus. You've been by my side this whole time." She then fixed her gaze on her three friends. "Thank you. You may think it was nothing, but it meant everything. I love you for it."

The group huddled together at first, and then Sarah hugged each of them individually. In that moment, when her arms tightened around him and her head nestled on his neck, Peter acknowledged there was no denying his feelings for Sarah. He could not prevent it, and he could not send it away. It was then he suspended his self-convicted life sentence, if only for a few seconds, and hugged Sarah back and placed his cheek on the top of her head.

The hug did not last conspicuously longer, nor did either of them awkwardly pull away when their eyes met upon separating. Although, Peter was very aware he could still feel her body against his well after the embrace was concluded.

David and Steven remarked to Sarah how courageous and inspirational she was to them and how her humbleness and gratefulness would stay with them for a long time to come. She deflected their compliments with simple thanks, and the group set back on their way toward the hotel.

Peter was grateful no one spoke to him for the rest of the walk. Once they returned, he quickly wished everyone a good night and excused himself to the lobby restroom.

THOMAS K. SHANNON

CHAPTER 28

It was daybreak by the time Peter Max re-entered the Marriott Eagle's Nest resort lobby. The sunrise behind him silhouetted his form as he walked through the revolving door and stepped onto the light pink marble. He was aware of his exhaustion and used his last moments of clear thought to ensure Sarah was not yet present. Once he confirmed her absence, he strode across the floor silently and disappeared down the hallway that led to the elevators.

As the elevator doors shut, he fell back against the rear wall and exhaled deeply while stretching his neck muscles from side to side. His eyes were unfocused, and his legs begged for rest. Indeed, rest was next on his agenda.

As he willed his way down the hallway toward his room, he had already started unbuttoning his shirt and was reaching for his belt buckle as his room key swiped the lock. Once inside, he athletically placed the "Do Not Disturb" banner on the outside door handle, and then his shirt, shoes, and pants were evacuated in record time.

His last motion, while his pants fell to the ground and he collapsed onto the bed, was to pull his hand from his pants pocket and place the necklace with the silver cross with beveled edges on the nightstand beside him. His lips formed a satisfied smile as he quickly drifted off to sleep.

When Peter next opened his eyes, he fixed them upon the blurred red numbers on the nightstand clock. Once in focus, they read 1:18 pm. He rolled himself over to confirm it was daytime and spied sunlight, slicing between the heavy curtains and drawing a line on the carpet beneath. He settled back into the middle of the bed and faced the ceiling while contemplating what came next.

His only goal the night before was to find her cross. But now that he had found it, he had to consider alternative ways to get it back to her. Most importantly, he had to consider how Sarah would react and how he would respond. Preparation was a must. He could not be surprised by any scenario. He must control the situation, especially now that his feelings were dissolving his guard. A part of him disliked the last 24 hours, and made him uncomfortable. But, a part of him also rejoiced every time he thought of Sarah, and it was gaining strength.

Peter repeated the night's highlights several times and paused on the shared glances and smiles. He replayed Sarah's words and touched as the evening progressed. However, each time he recounted the moment she realized the grace of her loss, the meaning she relayed through her grandmother's words, and the joy on her face when she thanked her friends, and the embrace they shared for moments that still lingered, he was overwhelmed by his want to absorb the pure and joyous feelings that swept over him. Each time it came, he allowed a bit more time to embrace it. However, each time, his commitment to his own apathetic sentence thwarted his desire and smothered his feelings...just as they had for over eight years. He had become quite practiced at it.

At 2:23 pm, Peter rose from the bed and got ready. His emotional state was chosen, as was his course of action.

Peter Max entered the lobby from the guest elevators at 3:08 pm. His face was clean-shaven, and his hair styled. For the first time in any length of time, he crafted an outfit from his available wardrobe. His pressed white shirt was tucked into his jeans, and his leather belt matched the color of his casual brown-laced shoes. However, the piece of clothing he felt best about was the navy striped blazer that accentuated his jeans and shoes. Inside the right-side pocket of his blazer was the necklace, Sarah's necklace. He tried every inside and outside pocket of the blazer inside his room before confirming the right-side pocket was the best choice for a smooth presentation.

He wanted to easily reach and extract her necklace without ever having to take his eyes off Sarah's face. His reward for inspecting the cobblestoned route until daybreak would be her eyes when she understood what was happening. That is all he wanted in return. To witness her look upon her most cherished possession. It was a possession that had nothing to do with material worth but still held immeasurable value for Sarah Garrity. When she shared her gratitude for the thoughtless love she received the night before, her comments slashed through Peter's shields. They were immediately absorbed directly into the very core of his being—gratitude expressed during a time of deep loss. There was no defense and no mindset that could repel it. From that moment, all he wanted was to return the feeling and watch her eyes explode with joy.

He felt more alive than he could ever recall.

As he crossed the lobby, Peter scanned the space for Sarah. Given the time of day, he did not expect to find her in the lobby area, but he thought it was the best place to start. He continued to walk toward the restaurant area, but he knew the night staff, including the chef, would not be in for another forty-five minutes.

He exited through the patio doors and found himself on the same balcony overlooking the pool area. Walking toward the rail, he noticed through its glass that Steven and Sarah were conversing on the path below. The first thing that caught his eye was Steven's well-chosen outfit: a soft tan sport coat over a medium blue un-tucked golf shirt expensive jeans with brown leather loafers. Suddenly, Peter felt a bit awkward and calculating.

Next, he noticed Steven's animated gestures as he spoke to Sarah and the complete attention she offered him. Steven's impassioned delivery lasted for an extended period, and Peter could surmise he was being serious and sincere from his body language. Steven's hands jutted forward and back, his back arched and fell, and his head dipped and straightened as he spoke. Sarah smiled at times and lost all expression at others, but she listened intently to his message. Finally, Steven's hand reached into his left side jacket pocket and produced a small black box.

Peter's hands instinctively gripped the top of the railing when he saw the box. What was going on here? What was in the box?!

As Steven's right hand pulled open the lid, Sarah stared down at the box. Immediately, Sarah's hands rose to cover her mouth. From her reaction, Peter knew what was inside before Sarah leaped forward to hug Steven affectionately. Steven's arms gently and then firmly closed around Sarah's back and his head fell between her shoulder and neck.

Peter watched intently for signs of deceit or fraud from Steven and/or obligation or politeness from Sarah- any sign. There were none to be witnessed. As he stood motionless above, he became intently aware of the rush of despair and envy that tackled his spirit and enraged him. Frozen in place as a spectator, he looked on as the hug separated, and Steven removed the cross from the box and went behind Sarah to drape it across her neck and clasp it in place. Sarah smiled brightly, and her right hand caressed the gift on her chest.

Before Peter willed his grip from the rail, he watched Sarah's eyes well with joy. It was then he fully realized the joy he wanted to see in her eyes was meant to be a gift for him alone. It was for him all along. Now that he saw it brought on by another, he felt ashamed that his reaction was deep anger and resentment. He turned in place and silently removed himself from the scene. He needed to find a place away from humanity where he could torture himself for his envy.

CHAPTER 29

It was after 7:00 pm when Peter re-entered the Eagle's Nest lobby. His time away from everyone and everything did little to change his anguish. He had walked in several different directions and sat on numerous benches and small walls over the last three and a half hours, desperately trying to empty his mind and numb his feelings.

From beginning to end, his failure to do so only contributed to his frustration. It did not help that Steven had called him four times without leaving a message. Only when he received Steven's text did he drop his useless efforts and head back to the hotel. Steven's text read: "Where are you? I'm leaving tonight."

Steven was sitting in a lobby chair, facing the entrance's revolving door, when Peter entered through them. The friend's eyes locked, but not before Peter spied Steven's packed luggage beside his chair. He also noticed the grateful expression on Steven's face as he closed the distance between them.

"You're leaving?" Questioned Peter.

"Yes."

"Where?"

"Back to Connecticut."

"Why?"

Although Steven immediately knew his reply, he paused to ensure he only needed to say it once, "I'm ready. I found what I was searching for."

Peter's expression clearly displayed what he was going to say. "I'm really confused. What are you talking about? What were you searching for?"

Before Steven responds, Peter adds, "I saw you gave Sarah the necklace. I saw your hug. I saw her smiling. I could tell you were being genuine."

Steven processed what Peter confessed, which made his explanation much easier. "Last night changed me."

"Last night?"

"The cross…Sarah's story…Her grandmother…Sarah's explanation and outlook. It changed me. It slapped me right across my face and shook me to my soul."

Peter completely understood what Steven described but still

found it difficult that someone else was as affected as he was by the event. Curiously, he asked, "How did it change you?"

"For a split second, I was able to see myself. It was a moment of complete revelation. And I was blown away. I despised what I saw. The man who stood in that alley was someone I hated recognizing. I saw what the last fifteen years, especially the last nine since the accident, have done to my character. I compensated for my guilt by caring only about my immediate satisfaction and the use of others for my immediate benefit. I was laid bare at that very moment, and I realized I was completely unworthy of the gratitude Sarah was offering me."

Steven smiled, then continued, "I was so shaken up, I couldn't talk, and honestly, it was hard for me even to walk back to the hotel. I went right up to my room when we got back, and I sobbed uncontrollably. Then, after what seemed like hours, I smiled. I smiled! I was suddenly filled with happiness. It was as if I had shed the chains of Jacob Marley! My emptiness was now overflowing. My worthlessness was given meaning. My heart leaped, and all I could think about was how lucky I was to be given such grace! Amazing grace! I was changed right there where I stood."

Peter absorbed every word his friend told him and knew they were absolutely true. Still, there was a loose end he needed to address. He reached for Steven's forearm and guided him into an area that would seemingly provide more privacy. "But Sarah?"

Steven smiled again and looked into Peter's eyes reassuringly. "This afternoon, I apologized to her. And I thanked her."

"The new necklace?" questioned Peter.

This morning, as soon as the shops opened, I called jewelry stores and described the cross based on what you had said. It took me seven tries, but finally, one could forward me a picture that looked very similar. I had them send it over by courier immediately, and I spent the rest of the day preparing what I would tell Sarah."

"And that was?" Petitioned Peter.

"I told her pretty much what I just told you. I said I was sorry for making her a part of my narcissism. She should never be objectified. She is so much more. She actually teared up a bit when I told her that. I told her she inspired me and that her words and actions caused something beautiful to occur inside me. I told her my whole being wished we could meet again and I could show her how a gentleman should act. Unfortunately, I knew I had much work to do before showing her that. But one day, I'll be ready to be her true friend and respect her in the way she deserves. I told her to let me know if I can ever do anything for her."

The words flowed excitedly from Steven's mouth, and he paused to check in with Peter, "Am I making any sense?"

"Perfect sense," confirmed Peter. "It looked like she loved the cross."

Steven lowered his eyes and confidently laughed as he remembered what she said. He looked at Peter again and finished the story by adding, "She told me she loved that the cross saved me. She told me losing her grandmother's gift turned out to be the most wonderful investment because it served its intended purpose. She said she was thrilled for me and would accept my gift as a new beginning with a new purpose."

Peter's hand touched the outside of his side pocket containing the original necklace. After slightly hesitating, he aggressively embraced his friend and spoke directly into his ear, "Steven, I am so happy you told me all of this, and I am even happier you indeed found what you were searching for!" The two separated, but Peter kept his hands firmly on Steven's shoulders. "It's been a long, dark ride."

Steven recognized that Peter was speaking of both of their journeys. He placed his arms on top of Peter's and nodded his head. "But now comes the light. Boy, I am going to enjoy this part."

The two embraced again quickly, then separated. Sensing it was time to move on, Peter asked, "What time is your flight?"

Steven did not need to look at his watch. "Oh, I missed it. I'll catch one tomorrow. I'll head toward a hotel near the airport tonight.

Stay as long as you want. My card is still in your room."

"You missed your flight waiting for me?"

"I wasn't leaving without seeing you, jackass," Steven paused. He found it amusing that after the previous few minutes of confession, he suddenly felt awkward. "Piper, I love you. And I want to thank you. I'm so, so sorry for what happened to Melissa and Anna. I've carried them and Lisa with me every day since. But I want to thank you for coming on this trip with me. I needed it...desperately. Today, I feel different than I have in a very long time. I'm ready to live outwardly, helpfully, curiously, and intentionally...with and through other people. I believe it's what's best for me because it's what would represent them best. Anyway, I'm going to begin with that as my purpose." Steven stopped and nodded once, then returned to his bags and picked them up. He walked back toward Peter and stood in front of him once again.

He spoke to Peter in a measured pace and tone, "Unlock your chains and let them fall off. I know you also have the key now. Open yourself up again."

Peter thought he needed to reply, but Steven grinned and walked toward the revolving door and the waiting cab outside.

"Who is gonna return the Porsche?" was the first thing Peter could think of saying out loud. Of course, he knew that was a defense. He sat quietly in the chair recently vacated by Steven and gazed forward for several minutes. Suddenly, he stood straight and adjusted his jacket. Peter then walked to the front desk and returned the smile of the waiting clerk.

"Hello, Christy."

"Hello, sir. How may I be of service?"

"I need a large envelope."

"Let me see what I have in the office...just one moment."

"Thank you."

Christy reappeared with a large manila envelope and handed it to Peter. Peter took the necklace from his side pocket, placed it into the envelope, peeled the tape from the flap, and sealed it. "Now, Christy, would you be so kind as to write 'Sarah Garrity' on the front of the envelope and place it in her mail?"

"Yes, sir."

"I'll wait while you write."

Christy smiled nervously as she wrote Sarah's name on the envelope. "Anything else, sir?"

Peter placed a $50 bill on the front desk. "Thank you for your help, Christy. That's all I want."

"Thank you, sir! Have a great night!" Christy said gratefully as she slid the tip toward her and watched the customer walk toward the guest elevators.

It was 11:15 pm when Peter once again entered the lobby with his bags in hand. As he approached, he was pleased to see the night clerk was now at the desk.

"Good evening, sir. How may I be of service?"

"Good evening, Tim. My name is Peter Max. I am checking out. I'll need my car brought around."

CHAPTER 30

The St. Francis Knights began their basketball season with two away games against non-conference opponents. Almost nine months ago, Peter requested the school's Athletic Director to schedule the games shortly after winning the championship. While providing fairly easy wins, the games were meant to shake the championship hangover for his seven returning seniors and identify challenges before taking on the area's more talented teams.

Today, the Knights were at home playing the last strategic opponent he had requested. The Edmonson Cardinals were well coached, but the school placed most of its athletic emphasis on lacrosse and soccer. Peter knew they would be athletic and competitive but were too short for his team. After the third quarter, the Knights led by only four points, and Peter was forced to play his starters for much longer than he anticipated.

Peter kneeled in front of his bench, and the players focused on him as he spoke. "Look, you've gotta dig deep. Take deep breaths and focus on the things that matter most, the things we talk about, and go over them every day in practice. Possession – we need to get a shot every time down the floor. Defense – we jump to the ball. Rebounding – everyone gets a body, and they only get one shot. Free Throws – same routine every time. We only have three team fouls this half. We can play a little more aggressively, but no reaching. Look for them to launch some threes. We have the advantage underneath. Steve, I want you to D up number 12… deny him the ball, and make him dribble before he shoots. Bobby, do not let 25 go baseline…your help is in the middle. Make him turn, understood? On offense, let's be patient, and if they overplay that pass to the wing, jab and go back door. Jack, I need you to think about offensive rebounds. Keep running the sequences; anyone can take a shot if it's open. Every one of you can score. You have to want this… want the ball, take the game right at them. Take the game right out of their hands and put them away. All right, everybody in."

Peter stood, turned, and faced mid-court as his team huddled at the bench and extended their hands into the center. Coach Max could hear Ryan, his 12th man, callout, "Let's go, Knights, take it right at them! On three…One, two …" and his teammates shouted "Knights!" in unison. The huddle broke open, and the St. Francis starting five ran onto the court at the same time Edmonson broke their huddle.

Three minutes into the fourth quarter, St. Francis' shooting forward got hot and hit three straight jump shots behind the arc, and the Knights led by thirteen points. Four minutes in, the lead grew to eighteen, and Coach Max was able to begin substitutions. He was sure to get his vocal leader, Ryan, some playing time, as well.

Once in the locker room, Peter congratulated his team for their tenacity and progress. He made sure to mention the upcoming schedule and start of conference games in the coming weeks. His team responded enthusiastically. Peter kept his talk short because it was a Sunday afternoon, and he wanted his players to spend some time with their families after a well-earned victory at home.

Peter exited the locker room and proceeded across the gym floor toward his office at the opposite end. As he walked, he greeted parents and students as they waited for their friends and sons. He repeated the obligatory "thank you" and "thanks for your support" many times. As he passed the last student, he mentally rejoiced over the clear path to his office door. But before his next step hit the floor, a voice behind him pointedly declared, "Your team gives up the baseline too much."

Several thoughts bombarded his brain, thoughts such as, "I can't say thank you or thanks for your support," or "No, duh! Who are you to tell me something like that? Where do you coach?" Should he offer back, "I agree. You're right. Good observation. I addressed it in our huddle. And we are working on it"? While he contemplated his response, he also struggled to place the voice. It sounded familiar, but he couldn't quite place it. Was it a player's mom? Maybe…but he tried hard never to speak with the parents… mother or father. Faculty member? Couldn't be…they knew better.

Peter staggered his steps as he pieced together this mental puzzle. Suddenly, he became anxious, and his stomach lurched inside him. He stopped awkwardly, almost against his will, and his eyes stared into the distance as he mouthed her name. "Sarah."

Peter pivoted slowly, and his eyes confirmed his belief. Sarah Garrity stood fifteen feet from him. The light from the setting sun streaming through the gym entrance shadowed her face, but he immediately knew it was her simply by the way she positioned herself.

"Sarah," he mustered. "I'm surprised. I'm excited to see you." As Peter spoke, he moved to the side so he could change the lighting and see her face more clearly. It showed the same nervous look he knew was on his own face. Sarah wore denim jeans that covered all but the foot of her boots. She was wearing boot heels on his court! Peter cursed himself for allowing his mind to go there, and he took note of her tan blazer over her white dress shirt. The silver belt buckle with a hint of turquoise combined the white with the denim in a dramatic fashion. His eyes moved upward again to her face. Her expression had not changed. It was then he noticed the St. Francis

Knights baseball hat atop her auburn hair.

Sarah replied, "I'm glad to hear you are excited because I didn't know how you would feel about seeing me again…especially unannounced."

"A coach's world is all about unannounced," replied Peter quickly. An awkward pause occurred, and the two smiled at each other.

"Nice hat," quipped Peter.

Sarah's eyes shot upward toward the brim of the cap. "I had to support the home team. How does it look?"

"Brand new. Like, you just flew into town and bought it in the bookstore."

"Exactly what I was going for."

"How did you know where to find me?"

Sarah shuffled her feet anxiously and answered sheepishly, "Turns out when you Google Peter Max…Baltimore, several articles on last season's championship come up. After that, I looked up your team schedule on the school's website."

"That almost seems too easy. Damn internet."

The two laughed lightheartedly and then stared at one another for an awkward amount of time. It was during those several seconds

Peter noticed the silver cross beneath Sarah's unbuttoned collar. It had to be the gift from Steven since he noticed it was subtly different than the original necklace he placed inside the large envelope. His mind darted from the present moment to the night in the alley, to the balcony view of Steven's presentation, to Steven's admission in the hotel lobby. Just as every memory flashed through his mind, so did his emotions as he reviewed them, rendering him even more anxious and uneasy. He could feel himself involuntarily swaying as he stood silent.

He could see Sarah's eyes tighten slightly as she also stood silently.

"Why did you leave?" she asked.

Peter fought his emotions and struggled to find his voice. He drew in his breath and answered as honestly as he knew how. "I was scared."

"Scared?"

"Scared... thrilled... petrified... sure...unsure...just plain dazed and confused. I was a complete whack job. I was going under, and I couldn't think straight. Hardly good company." Peter knew being honest would lead to her next question, but it was all he could think to do.

"What caused all of that?" Sarah required.

"I'm sorry I left without seeing you."

"That's not what I asked," Sarah shot back. "I kept telling myself for the last several months you didn't owe me anything... even a goodbye. We spent several days together and went to a baseball game. I do that with a lot of guests. Why would I expect something different from you? I kept telling myself that. But I never accepted it. It kept nagging me to know, and I kept telling myself to let it go. Finally, like the fool I am, I hopped a plane and bought this hat to ask you in person...why did you leave?"

"I answered you. Anxiety." Peter shifted his weight.

"And I asked you what caused you to feel that way?"

"A lot of things. Nothing in particular." Peter was aware his answers were curt and without substance, but it was all he would allow.

"Ok. So, I should have stayed in Phoenix. You clearly believe you didn't owe me anything," Sarah's words cut at Peter's cold exterior and opened a gap large enough for her next words to make an impact. "But I deserved better."

Purely on instinct, Peter replied, "What makes you think you deserved better?"

"This." Sarah reached into her jacket pocket and produced her grandmother's cross. She thrust her open hand toward Peter.

Peter looked into her hand and tried to stay emotionless. "Your necklace. I'm glad you found it. I see you have a new one now."

"I didn't find it," corrected Sarah. "You did."

Peter knew the answer before he asked, but he proceeded anyway. "Why do you think I found it?"

"Imagine my first action after receiving a large envelope addressed to me by Christy with my grandmother's cross inside. No note. What might I have done next, Peter?"

"Looked at the front desk camera footage," replied Peter as a statement.

"Bingo! I looked at the front desk footage. It didn't take very long for you to place it inside the envelope and have Christy address it. In fact, I looked at a bit of lobby footage from that same evening. I'm sure you can tell me what I saw, but I'll let you sit this one out. I saw you and Steven talking. Rather, I mostly saw Steven talking to you in the same excited, passionate way he had spoken with me earlier in the day. I have to imagine you know very well he gave me the cross I'm wearing now."

For a moment, Sarah paused briefly to let that information linger by itself.

Peter used the time to interject. "It didn't matter then, and it obviously doesn't matter now."

"What doesn't matter?"

"It doesn't matter that I looked for your necklace because it no longer matters to you. Steven told me you would wear the one he gave you." Peter's voice became agitated. He could feel his heart racing and his stomach tightening.

"That's why you left," Sarah concluded. Then, she questioned, "That's why you left?"

She could sense Peter was interpreting the situation very differently than she intended. She stepped toward him. Peter retreated at the same time.

"You know my back story," Peter said sharply, using the statement as a symbolic shield. "I didn't want any of this to happen. You standing here. Me looking for your necklace. I never wanted to get involved in any of this!" he said defiantly.

Sarah noticed that while his words were forceful, Peter's shoulders dropped as he finished. She stepped toward him again. This time, he stood still. Sarah placed her hand on his forearm and gently said, "Peter. It's life. And it was you being you. You cannot hold yourself to standards that contradict who you are...even if you mandate them. You looked for my cross because it's who you are. You also can't beat yourself up for having that inside you."

"No... You're wrong. I can definitely kick my ass for letting my emotions get away from me." Peter stood still and allowed her hand to rest on his arm. But he demanded of himself that he remain detached. "I spent the night looking for a stupid necklace you no longer wear. I went looking for you to surprise you with it, only to see you talking with Steven. Then, I found out the whole lost necklace thing changed him on the spot, and he genuinely confided in you. He got you a replacement necklace you prefer over your lost one. I saw the look of joy you gave him when he gave it to you."

Peter stopped talking and drew in a deep breath. Sarah tightened her hand on his forearm. He could sense she was about to say something, so he blurted out, "And I got jealous! Jealous! I hated seeing him with you, ok?! What an ass I am! I let down my guard and allowed myself to anticipate being happy, only to witness it be blown to pieces by my own stupidity. I was wrong! And I betrayed Melissa...again!" Peter's voice trembled.

Sarah spoke slowly and softly. "Peter, I want to explain some things that you are misunderstanding. I came here to..."

"Fix me!" accused Peter loudly. "That's what you do, right? You fix people. You fixed David from being a drunken bouncer after your boyfriend cracked his head open for stealing some beer at a field party..."

"What? What did David tell you about..." Sarah immediately

341

asked, but Peter was too focused on placing blame and did not even acknowledge her concern over his previous statement.

Peter continued, "You saved Steven on the spot with your gratitude and attitude and story about thoughtless love. Turned him from a womanizer to a stand-up guy who realized the error of his ways in a dark alley after the All-Star game! Who knows how many other lives you've saved! I'm sure the list goes on forever." Peter placed his hand on Sarah's and looked into her eyes. "Well, I'm a lost cause, Ms. Garrity...by choice. I don't deserve to be saved."

Keeping his hand on Sarah's, Peter lowered his forearm, broke the contact, and released her hand.

Sarah saw the redness in Peter's eyes as he finished. "I'm sorry I left without seeing you. I was jealous. I didn't see your eyes light up with joy when I returned your necklace. I was embarrassed that I was wrong about what it meant to you and what might happen between us after I gave it back to you. And I felt guilty as hell for betraying Melissa's memory. I have to go. Please let me."

A tear traced its way down Sarah's cheek as she watched Peter walk out of the gym and into the afternoon's darkening sky. She stared down at the cross still in her hand and wept.

CHAPTER 31

There was silence inside Peter's car, except for the sound of heavy rain smashing against its windshield and roof. He had driven away from the school without considering where he might go. When the rain began, it was torrential, and Peter became aware his mind was everywhere except on the road. He pulled into a convenience store parking lot to decompress and wait. He sat there listening to the rain while occasionally turning on his wipers to clear his view for the small increments of time. He was empty and numb.

The rain stopped as quickly as it started, and the sun's Fall rays slipped through the empty tree limbs, illuminating the drops on his windshield. Just as quickly, Peter's emptiness turned to regret and shame. He slithered down his car seat and plopped his head against the headrest. He extended his exhale and gripped the steering wheel as billows of exhaust smoke passed by his window.

For the first time in nine years, he acknowledged he was no longer in control of what he felt or how he would feel going forward.

His thoughts, as well as his actions, were overtaken by something he didn't see coming. Or, he thought, maybe he did see it coming but couldn't get out of its way. Or, perhaps, he didn't want to get out of its way. He overestimated himself or…underestimated the power of…love? No, it wasn't love. He repeated that thought in his mind. "No, it isn't love…No, it is not love…"

As he repeated it for the fourth time, Peter couldn't believe he was smiling. The fifth time he thought it, he added, "But it's still something pretty good!"

He sat up straight in his seat and drove out of the parking lot. He knew where he wanted to go. He had to go.

CHAPTER 32

Parklawn cemetery was never a destination Peter visited at the spur of the moment. In fact, his last visit was four years ago, when he accepted the coaching position at St. Francis. It was an update type of visit.

Peter pulled alongside the patch of green grass surrounded by trees, which served as Melissa and Anna's resting place. He turned off the car's engine and opened his door. The outside wind swirled inside the car as the door swung open. The rain brought chilly air. Still, he left his jacket behind and walked forward slowly through the wet grass toward the grave site. He noted how much the trees had grown since he was first there nine years ago. Time kept going, and things changed.

Peter stood six feet from the headstones and made note of the empty space beside them. When the time came, the plan was always to claim the space with his own headstone. He looked down upon their names and began by saying, "Hi, my loves."

Peter paused momentarily and considered if they knew why he had come to see them. They were in heaven, and that held certain perks, right? He decided they probably knew. Heck, they probably knew before he did. Finally, he decided whether they knew or not, he still needed to tell them himself.

"Sorry, I haven't been by in a long time. But you know I carry both of you with me every day. I think about you always. Seeing this place only reminds me of why you are here in the first place. God knows I don't need a reminder. I'm well aware of why you are here." Peter continued to stare at their names. "I'm sorry. With all that I am, I'm sorry."

A stiff breeze reminded Peter of the weather change, and he focused on Anna's name. "Anna...my darling girl. It's not lost on me that you'd be twelve now, but I'll always see you as you were when you were three...adorable. What three-year-old girl isn't adorable, right? But I need to tell you that. You are adorable...and funny, and kind, and loving. And I can't stand not being able to see you at twelve. I carry that with me, too. I want to tell you how much I love you and miss you. I remember bouncing you on my knee and drinking imaginary tea. I remember teaching you how to swing a bat and golf club and even catch a ball...you were a natural. I can remember your laugh. I remember how infectious it was...it made everyone laugh with you. And you laughed a lot. I remember how my heart would ache having to hear you cry when you got hurt.

Lucky for me, you hardly ever cried…you were tough. I remember you in your Easter dress and shiny black shoes. Most of all, I remember your bonnet and how beautiful you looked as I carried you into church. I remember the icing on your face when you ate cupcakes. I remember the look in your eyes after I would tell you 'no' and the look in your eyes when I eventually said 'yes'. It was always easy to say 'yes' to you, Anna. I remember you reaching up to hold my hand when we walked. And I remember your sweet voice when you'd whisper, 'I love you,' after I would tuck you in."

Peter had to stop and regain his composure. He continued, "I want to tell you I will never forget even a single one of those things. They are all I have of you…and more than I deserve. You were more than I deserved. I love you, Anna. And I know you loved me." Peter smiled as he kissed two of his fingers, stepped forward, and gently placed them over Anna's name.

He stepped back to focus on Melissa's name. His hands rubbed his face in preparation. Peter began, "Melissa. I came today to tell you I've failed…again. But some things have happened over the last few months that make me believe it was inevitable that I failed…and it was fortunate for me to fail." Peter stood up straight, then relaxed his stance once again.

"This is unrehearsed, so I have no idea how it may spill out or if I can even say it in a way that makes any sense. In fact, it could be that, as I say it, we both realize I'm full of shit. But I came here to say it to you, as I said it for the first time. You deserve to hear what is going through my head…and heart. Please bear with me. These are all new thoughts."

He considered where to begin and chose near the end. "I have feelings for Sarah Garrity. I'm assuming you know all about her, mostly because I'm assuming you hear what I'm saying; otherwise, I would be standing here trying to explain. See, I warned you this was unrehearsed. Anyway, I have feelings for Sarah. I'm here because I pledge never to allow myself to experience these feelings again. I believed if I denied intimacy, I'd honor your memory. Even more, by denying myself pleasure, I'd somehow pay my dues for being so selfish and stubborn. I never believed I was the direct reason you are gone…because it was an accident. It could have happened any time, any day. No, I sentenced myself because I was so consciously aware of how badly I took advantage of you that day that I would remind myself, at every chance, of my manipulation and ego. Steven and I could have gone to the store…we should have gone. What's crazy is no one needed to go to the store!" Peter stepped backward and sighed heavily, causing him to see his breath. He was becoming angry, which was not why he was visiting his family. He needed to control his mind and say his beliefs without getting distracted by negative emotions.

He began again. "I'm not going to tell you how much I loved

you. In a way, I just did. Which is fine; I'm not afraid to say it. Ok, I'll tell you. I loved you. I loved you with everything that I am. And I let you down because I placed myself and my career in front of my love for you. I felt a ton of guilt for it. I got the idea I would show you how much I loved you by denying myself and neglecting others. I was doing really well, too. Almost nine years without breaking a sweat." Peter placed his hands into his pockets. "Turns out, I did that for me, too. I never stopped being selfish. I wasn't denying myself so much as I was denying others...avoiding having to give of myself, protecting against having to love someone, anyone... everyone ever again. I believed if I could wait long enough, the pain of losing you would subside just enough so I could live with it. Hell, I wanted to embrace it. I longed to wrestle with it. Guilt was a small price to pay for my tab. But that's just it. I sentenced myself to something that was easy for me. I retreated into a corner and merely existed. There was no thought of living or what it meant to live. I existed. For a guy who is stubborn and selfish, that wasn't a sentence. It was a pardon!"

Peter stopped again to make sure he was OK with how he was presenting his thoughts to Melissa. Satisfied, he went on. "I took the worst part of my personal makeup and doubled down! You weren't there to tell me it was weak or self-centered. And I wouldn't allow anyone else near me to offer advice. It was the perfect plan for a guy like me."

Now, Peter was stopping every few lines. He needed to get his thoughts in line and not stray. "Melissa, I realized recently, I mean within the last few hours, that the opposite of stubborn and selfish is selflessly living for others…whatever the cost."

Peter stared at Melissa's name as if he expected a reply. After a few moments, he offered, "Did that come out right? I'm wondering myself because that's my main message…and it better not be bull shit." He continued to stare. "I mean, it's a new concept for me. I don't want to be back here next month explaining why it was all bullshit and asking you to forget I even said it."

Peter stated his message again. "The opposite of stubborn and selfish, the opposite of how I was living my life, my existence, is selflessness, charity, compassion, and service." He stood straighter and grinned. "I must be onto something, Melissa. I feel good every time I say it." Then, looking at the sky, he added, "And you haven't tried to hit me with a lightning bolt or anything! It's a joke, it's a joke! A little levity, that's all."

Peter looked again at the names carved in front of him, and his smile vanished. The lines on his forehead were creased, and his lips were pursed tightly against his teeth. He struggled to stop the feelings welling within him, and then, just as quickly, he decided to express them so Melissa and Anna could finally see what he was carrying with him for all those years. Peter's knees gave way, and he willingly kneeled before his family before falling forward and spreading his arms in an attempt to cradle the two graves. Peter Max wailed into the ground, and his entire body shook with grief.

THOMAS K. SHANNON

CHAPTER 33

The elevator doors opened, and Peter habitually proceeded forward and turned to his left toward his condo at the end of the hall. He had done the same ritual for nearly six years, so his body was pre-conditioned to take him to his door without thinking or focusing.

He was speaking into his phone as he walked. "Sarah, it's Peter Max. I'm sorry for leaving you so abruptly this afternoon and for the things I said. I'm hoping you are still in town and that you will check your voicemail before you leave. I need to speak with you. Please give me a call when you get this message. I'm at 410-555-3823. Please, I really want to talk with you."

As Peter finished his message and lowered his phone to end the call, his eyes caught the blurry figure sitting across the hall from his door. He hit the red button and directed his attention to the visitor. He walked deliberately, like a ship coasting into the harbor. He finally stopped ten feet from Sarah, who looked up at him with a puzzled smile, trying to understand why the front of his shirt and pants had gotten so wet and stained. She decided that was unimportant and confirmed she heard him talking as he walked the hallway. "I got your message," she said. "What do you want to talk about?"

"How did you know where I live?" Peter asked, truly surprised to find her waiting for him.

"You filled out the guest registration when you checked into the Eagle's Nest," offered Sarah.

"Aaaahhh. I never pictured you a stalker," Peter responded with fake concern.

"You could get me fired, I suppose. Breach of customer privacy."

"I'll keep it as an option. How did you get into the building without a fob?" asked Peter curiously.

"I chatted up a nice young man with a St. Francis sweatshirt. When I told him I knew you and would surprise you after flying in from Phoenix, he was very kind to let me follow him in."

"Easy mark, those teenage boys. I'll also have a chat with Billy Jones about building security at school tomorrow." Peter extended his hand to help Sarah to her feet. As she rose, he wondered admirably, "I'm surprised you didn't pick my lock and make yourself at home."

Sarah stood straight and locked onto his eyes. "A woman doesn't show all her abilities at once. Besides, some may think that was going a bit far."

Peter smiled genuinely as he looked down into Sarah's hazel eyes. They stood facing each other briefly, and then Peter motioned toward his door. "Would you like to come in?"

"No, thank you," Sarah confidently answered. "If this visit doesn't go well, leaving from here will be less awkward than leaving your living room."

"Point taken. You don't seem to have a problem with having personal conversations out in the open," observed Peter.

Sarah looked down both ends of the hallway. "Other than me and you, no one has come down the hallway in over an hour. Besides, I don't know your neighbors, and they don't know me." She looked back at Peter and said plainly, "Let's have a talk."

Peter did not hesitate. Her request was met with his immediate response. "I'm broken."

He thought his statement would get a reaction. Instead, Sarah waited in anticipation.

He repeated his opening statement, "I'm broken...and I don't expect you to fix me."

"Stop!" It was clear Sarah was waiting for that specific

accusation, and this time. She would not let it pass. "I want to make something clear. I don't fix people! I'm not looking for that, and I don't want the job. Here's a news flash, Peter…we are all broken! You can go up and down this hallway and every hallway in this building, floor after floor, condo after condo, and everyone is broken! It's part of being human. Even when you thought you were fine, you were broken! Our makeup is flawed. We aren't perfect. We can never be perfect. But we can keep getting better…keep supporting each other…keep being grateful and giving thanks… keep searching for others to help…and help ourselves in the process." Sarah took a quick breath, not wanting to be interrupted.

She continued, "If you think I hang around people who needed fixing, it's because they did. But you know what? They are getting better…on purpose. They want to get better. And they let me in. They allow me to be their friend, and I love…I cherish…that I can support them, and they support me." Sarah stopped, emphasizing, "Peter, I'm broken, too."

"Sarah, I said some things this afternoon that were flat-out wrong. Basically, everything I said this afternoon was flat-out wrong." Peter added, "When I saw you, I was surprised, and I immediately went into a panic. My first thought was to run toward you and hug you, but my defense was to retreat and deflect from any honest conversation because what I wanted to say did not come close to matching my determination to get out of that place. It overwhelmed me. All the feelings I had when we were in Phoenix came rushing back, and I got scared...again. I acted like a fool, and I'm sorry."

"It seems you have taken the time to think it through?"

"Yes."

"And?"

"And I..." Peter considered if he should share where he went and what he did. Was it really necessary? Would it add to anything, or would it subtract? Did it even mean anything? "Will you indulge me for a minute?"

Sarah tilted her head slightly and quizzically peered at him. "I have some time."

"Good. I'm not stalling...just getting my bearings." Peter clasped his hands in front of him. "When we first met, I was steadfast in my lack of interest in anything resembling a relationship. You felt the same way, correct?'

"Yes." Sarah thought about saying more but decided she was indulging him. He should talk.

"At some point, I don't care where or when I began to fight back the urge to become friends. Maybe you didn't fight your feelings, but you consciously decided that we were getting along pretty well, right?"

"Yes."

Peter nodded. "Skip a couple of steps. I spent the night finding your necklace, and you hopped a flight to Baltimore because we actually do care about one another?" Peter gestured for her to acknowledge his question with an answer.

Sarah's eyes shifted, and she resisted smiling. "Yes."

"Ok. Ok." Peter turned on his heel and walked several steps down the hall as his fingers cupped his mouth. He spun back toward her and stepped forward again. "Ok!" he announced, and Sarah knew he had confirmed everything he needed to proceed. "After I left you, I drove around in the rain and had to pull over to think. My mind was so full… it was blank. I know that sounds stupid, but I couldn't concentrate on anything but the rain hitting my windshield." Peter looked at Sarah to see if he had lost her. She looked back at him in anticipation.

"What happened, in that moment, was that with my mind so preoccupied, I finally understood what my entire being wanted! Not even wanted…craved! I was so empty inside I was starving. I was dying." Peter looked directly at Sarah. "I finally figured out I don't want to die this way, the way I am, who I am."

Sarah absorbed everything Peter was confiding in her and resisted the urge to interrupt. Peter continued, "I don't know exactly what we mean to each other. I'm unsure if our relationship goes anywhere, or stops dead in its tracks, after we learn about each other. I've never over-estimated, counted my chickens, or got my hopes too high…but I know this…I want to know more about you. I want to know everything about you because what I've come to know up to this point has caused me to blow up and redefine everything I convinced myself to believe!"

Peter quietly checked his status with Sarah. "This is the point when I need to ask if you think I'm crazy or unhinged because I'm very aware that you could, with cause." He waited for a response that took too long. "Do you think I'm insane?"

She did not look him in the eye and instead gazed straight ahead, seemingly in deep thought. Finally, she reported, "I'm following you, and I share many of the same feelings, and no, I do not think you are insane, unhinged, or crazy. Please know I am listening intently to everything because I want to learn more about you. But, there is something I've been meaning to ask you since you arrived, but the timing didn't seem right."

"Anything," Peter offered. "What do you want to know?"

Sarah did not avert her gaze. She methodically raised her hand and pointed toward his shirt. "Why are your clothes so stained with grass and dirt?"

Peter jerked his head downward to follow her finger to the dried stains on his shirt and pants. Once out of the chilled air and into his heated car, his clothes dried, and he had forgotten about his appearance.

"Oh, that." He struggled for a transition. "Actually, this helps get me to the next part of my confession."

"Please. I'm all ears." Sarah cajoled, keeping the mood light.

"Let's get this out of the way. After the rain stopped and I had my revelation, I went to the cemetery and ended up flat on my face, trying to hug my late wife and daughter." He shrugged his shoulders. "Yeah, I really did that. It wasn't on my list of things to do when I got there, but at the time, it became necessary. So, to back up a bit...I went to visit Melissa and Anna to explain myself and introduce you. Before I could do anything else, I needed to ensure they heard my story directly from me. I hoped they would understand, and although I didn't hear them answer, I'm confident I received their answer. They would have never sentenced the burden of apathy on me. I did that. They would not have wanted that as a testament to their memories. They were loving people and would be angry with me for shutting myself off from loving others. I went to explain and apologize. And, while I was there, I needed to tell them I was feeling something for another person." Peter looked slyly at Sarah. "Something more than friendship."

"How did that go? Any lightning?"

"That's what I said!" exclaimed Peter, his hands darting

toward Sarah. "No. No lightning. I felt a tremendous weight lifted from me, and for the first time in so long, I felt their love and embrace. At that moment, I had no choice but to get as close as I could to them, so I fell to my knees and then to the ground and cried as I hugged them back."

Sarah inadvertently let out a small gasp, and her cupped hands went to her lips. Peter added, "It was the first time I cried over them." His right hand went to his eyes, and his thumb and forefinger were wiped across his eyes. He let out an embarrassed laugh. "Oh man, it's been one hell of a day…a very enlightening day, to say the least. What an idiot I've been." He took a half step toward Sarah. "Anyway, after I let out nine years of mourning, I picked myself up, dried myself off, and began calling every Marriott in a 40-mile radius trying to find you, only to find you 'breaking and entering' into my building."

"Hardly 'breaking and entering'."

"Maybe not…but definitely loitering."

"Fair enough."

The two stood in the hallway, facing each other, and the awkward silence they were trying to avoid finally invaded the scene. A few moments passed, and Peter spoke again. "What happens next?"

Sarah responded, "I need to explain some things to you as well."

Peter's eyes widened. He didn't expect her to explain anything. She didn't need to. But he was thrilled she felt like she could.

"But, before I do..." she added, "...can we sit down? My feet hurt." Sarah gestured toward the floor against the wall where Peter first found her. They both sat next to each other, facing his door.

"I'm all ears," announced Peter. Sarah smiled silently, acknowledging his imitation.

"When I told you I was broken, too...it wasn't a line." She hesitated, organizing the order in which she wanted to address her topics. "I want to tell you about how and when I met David... my grandmother's cross... Steven's gift... and why I came to Baltimore." Sarah repositioned her body slightly so she could see Peter as she spoke. He did likewise.

"David didn't end up in the hospital for stealing beer at a field party. They hit him with that bottle after he stopped my boyfriend from trying to rape me." Sarah saw Peter's eyebrows raise, and he bit his lower lip slightly. She paused for a second to let his mind digest what he had just learned.

"It's true that David and his friends showed up to the party a little drunk and asked if they could get a beer. The jocks, who were also lit, took it as an opportunity to get the underclassmen shit-faced and then embarrass them, so they quickly agreed and even poured them large cups of beer. Then, the drinking games started. The jocks didn't think David and his friends would last as long as they did or be as good as they were at the games. Their plan backfired, and after a couple of hours, everybody was drunk, including the jocks... including my boyfriend. At one point, he stumbled over to where I was sitting, and after three tries, I finally convinced him to leave. We only made it thirty yards or so through the woods, heading back to his car, when he sat on a rock and grabbed me. At first, he tried to kiss me playfully, and I kissed him back a couple of times. But when I tried to convince him I wasn't interested and went to leave, things stopped being playful. I won't go into details, but we ended up on the ground with him on top of me. I was no match for him, even with him being so drunk. Everything you hear about helplessness doesn't do justice to what I felt. I can remember every detail of what was happening and every detail of my pleas for him to stop."

Sarah paused out of necessity. She was being transported back to those moments and sequence of events, and she felt every emotion that accompanied her thoughts welling inside her. She blinked twice and slightly shook her head as she regained her focus on Peter, who had never stopped studying her.

"Sarah, if this is too painful, I don't need to know anymore." Peter meant it.

"I need you to know." Sarah stiffened her body. "I am fine...thank you. Enter David, who I learned later had heard the struggle and my protests when he entered the woods to go to the bathroom. Funny, I can remember the rustling sound he made as he ran toward our location, but I never considered anyone was coming to help me. I was so convinced I was going to be raped that I gave up hope. The last thing I remember is David's eyes locked onto mine as he reached us. I could barely make him out through my tears, but I could see the rage in his face. David grabbed my boyfriend by his arms and lifted him off me, then placed his arm around his neck and pulled him backward. My boyfriend was stunned, but when he realized what was happening, he broke free and tried to punch David wildly. David used his inertia to throw him against the rock and began beating him repeatedly until he slumped to the ground, unconscious."

Peter's back was stiff against the wall. "I'm sorry that happened. I have no idea what that must have been like."

"After so many years, I've never been able to describe it with any combination of words...real or made up. Thank you. That scene is now out of the way, except for important details. I also need to share them with you because they all relate to why we are sitting here now."

"Please." With one word, Peter told her he would listen to everything she had to say.

"It's true. David got hit with a full bottle of vodka, and he ended up in the hospital. The jocks heard my struggle too, and my boyfriend's yelling when he and David were fighting. Funny, I didn't hear them coming through the woods. David was still bent over my boyfriend when one of the jocks ran up from behind and hit him as hard as he could with the bottle. It didn't break. David crumpled to the ground. Everyone thought he was dead, including the jocks, who ran away, back to their cars, and left. David's friends helped me get both unconscious bodies back to my boyfriend's car, and I told them to go home, sober up, and stay out of it. I'd take them to the hospital…which I did. It turns out that it didn't matter that they left because the cops and the school administration agreed that no charges would be made since we had been dating for over six months. The incident was probably normal sexual drive after too many beers, and they couldn't identify the person who hit David because I wasn't an unbiased witness. They all graduated as planned." Sarah looked down at the floor and shook her head in disgust. "They decided not to ruin their college sports careers over a field party fight." She let out a soft, sarcastic laugh.

She looked at Peter, bringing herself mentally back to the

hallway. "I spent the summer in my room and developed an eating disorder. The only productive thing I did, with the help of my parents, was to switch my college choice to a school on the West Coast, as far from my high school as possible. This brings me to my grandmother - She had kept tabs on me after the incident but, at the request of my parents, stayed at arm's length for most of the summer while I went to therapy. Finally, a week before I was to leave for school, she asked me to go to lunch. Afterward, she asked if I would pray with her. I told her I didn't have much use for prayer. She asked why, and without even the slightest hesitation, I said, 'Because God abandoned me.' My grandmother stopped walking and took my hand in hers. She looked at me lovingly and asked, 'Have I abandoned you?' Talk about a haymaker! Her question was so unexpected my knees buckled, and my eyes filled with tears. I told her, in a tone several times louder than my normal voice, "Mom-mom, I adore you! You would never abandon me! You have always been my biggest ally; I know you love me. I know my parents asked you to give me space, but I always knew you were there for me and would do anything for me!"

Sarah looked both ways down the hall, thinking her loud voice might cause some doors to open. When she was confident that they would remain closed, she continued, "All my grandmother said back was, 'Then let me pray for you'. So, off we went to the church, which 'not so coincidentally', was two blocks from where she took me to lunch."

"Smart grandmother," injected Peter.

"Indeed. Smart grandmother," Sarah agreed. "We sat silently in the church pew for about ten minutes. I tried to do anything but pray. In fact, I wanted to completely ignore God. I wanted Him to think I didn't even care enough to acknowledge Him in any way. So, I sat there and looked at the ceiling, the candles, and the organ pipes. I counted the pews and tried to figure out the church's seating capacity...anything to keep my mind off God." Sarah put her head against the wall behind her. But I couldn't. Instead, I blamed Him. I told Him he left me to get raped. I accused him of forgetting about me. I challenged him to tell me why I deserved to be raped...what did I do to deserve His punishment?"

Sarah's words came out in staccato fashion, and her breathing sped up. "My anger wasn't enough, though. I went through every detail with Him. Falling to the ground, having my boyfriend on top of me, being unable to move him off me, feeling his hands fumble with my clothes while he rubbed my body through them. Repeating to God what he was saying to me. 'Relax...you're fine...what's wrong with you? Stop saying no. Be quiet! C'mon, you're going to like it.' I knew God had heard it all before. My story wasn't new...it didn't differ in any way from the thousands of other women who heard the same things while lying powerlessly and processing what was happening to them. Thinking about that only made me angrier because I knew God couldn't tell me why all those women deserved to be raped. Even if He told me they didn't deserve it, He allowed it to happen! He was complicit! Why did I need God for anything when my boyfriend was the one who needed God?! God didn't have to protect me…but why didn't He change Mark's mind?!"

Keeping her head against the wall, Sarah exhaled, and her demeanor quickly changed. She turned to face Peter. "I don't believe that anymore," she said calmly. "But that is a discussion for another time."

She returned her head to its previous position. "As I was silently screaming at God, I felt my grandmother's hand on mine. I was rubbing my thigh so fast and hard through my jeans that she was concerned I was going to rip a hole in them. She looked at me and asked, 'Do you believe He is listening?' Mom-Mom, I don't care if He is listening. I know He isn't answering! He never answers me!"

Sarah reached into her pocket and brought out her grandmother's cross. She held open her hand, and it hung from her fingers. "My grandmother held my hand even firmer. She told me, 'Sweet Sarah…it is ok to tell Jesus you are angry. You must…you must tell him you don't understand how he could allow such things to happen. If you hate Him, you must tell Him that, too! It is the best way to clear your mind so He can answer you. Jesus knows how you feel.

He also knows what is in your heart. It is you who needs to listen. You cannot force yourself to hear Him, but He speaks to you in so many ways.' She held my face and caressed it. 'It is good that you are angry with God because it means you believe in Him. You couldn't be angry with Him if you believed he didn't exist. Please don't shun Him. Present your anger so He can replace it with His grace. You may not recognize it or be ready to accept it, but one day, you will recognize His grace.' My grandmother then put her hand forward with this crucifix in it. She continued by asking if I would wear it as a sign that my heart was open to Him. She said, 'As you go and live your life, every time you look upon it, it will remind you that Jesus sacrificed himself for the sole purpose of having a conversation with you. The cross reminds us that even in what should have been a symbol of failure and despair, lies the truth about love and triumph.' I nodded that I would wear it, and she placed it around my neck."

Sarah turned her head back toward Peter. "As we walked out of the church, she told me, 'Christ allowed himself to be tortured as an act of thoughtful love. You have been subjected to an act of thoughtless disregard for love. I asked the Lord to keep you close until a time of His choosing when He would present Himself to you through an act of thoughtless..."

"Love," finished Peter.

Sarah smiled at him and confirmed, "You know the rest of the story."

Peter smiled back at Sarah. "I do." He stared at his own door and was amused at how it came to be that he had that particular view. He added, "It was the most amazing example of personal cognisance I have ever witnessed in my entire life. I have never been present when someone released something so sentimentally valuable to them with such...contentment." He turned back to Sarah. "I found it as powerful as a sledgehammer...except, instead of damaging me, it did the complete opposite...it fortified my spirit. That moment, that scene, completely shattered my way of thinking."

Sarah raised her hand, holding the cross toward Peter. "I want you to have it," she said softly.

Peter stared into her open hand, then at the cross around her neck. Sarah followed his eyes and explained, "When I accepted Steven's gift, my grandmother's cross was lost...gone. He asked me to wear his gift in its place and pray that he would become the type of man deserving of admiration. He told me that when he could be admired, he could then seek love and return love."

She closed her fingers tightly around the chain so only the crucifix draped from the side of her palm. "Imagine how I felt when I opened the anonymous envelope, and this fell into my hand! I was undone. I was filled with joy and wonder at the same time. I felt God

371

right there beside me. He had shown me His love the night before… and the very next morning… showed me how He worked through me to show others a path to a more fulfilling life."

Her left hand reached up to touch the cross around her neck. "Of course, I would wear Steven's gift and pray for him." Her right hand re-opened, and she raised it again toward Peter. "I also knew God returned this to me to use as a reminder to someone else that He loves them."

Peter looked upon her hand and said meekly, "But it is your grandmother's and yours. I can't…"

"We want you to have it. Will you wear it?"

"Always."

Sarah turned her body toward him as her hands opened the clasp and spread the chain. Peter bowed his head forward, and she fastened it around his neck. He raised his left hand and held it delicately. He looked gratefully at the ceiling and then at Sarah. "Thank you to your grandmother and you for this unbelievable gift. It is unbelievable because no one could have convinced me I'd be wearing a cross yesterday. Even more, I don't ever want to take it off."

"Once again, I am filled with joy, Peter. Thank you!" Sarah wrapped her arms around his shoulders and pulled him close. He instantly responded by placing his arms around her and pulling her tight. Their heads rested on each other's shoulders, and they both exhaled heavily. They held each other for several moments, securing their grasp.

They separated and fell back onto the wall, replaying the conversation from the last several minutes as their breathing returned to normal. "Sarah?" requested Peter.

Without moving, she responded, "David."

Peter nodded slightly and asked, "I get why he wouldn't tell me the whole story. He didn't know me at all, and he was protecting you."

"I'm sure that is why he told you what he did," she agreed.

"His story after…?" Peter inquired.

"Pretty accurate," she responded. "He joined the Marines, worked as a bouncer, got into drugs and alcohol, and eventually into a lot of fights."

"And you sought him out?"

"Yes. After I healed, I tried to reconnect and tell him how grateful I was for what he did for me. I never really thanked him before I left for school. I tracked him to some dive bar. He wasn't too appreciative that I just showed up one night to 'thank' him after being away so many years." Sarah stopped, then started again, "In fact, he told me he would have done it for a dog and to get the fuck out of his sight. Yeah, that's what he said."

"Didn't catch him on a good night, I guess,"

"Sarah grinned and added, "He wasn't any better the next night or the next couple of weeks. Finally, I didn't go back for a week, and he showed up at the hotel where I was working in Personnel. We didn't say a word to each other. We both knew."

"Been together ever since, huh?"

"Pretty much."

"Two attractive people…"

"I guess," replied Sarah, nonchalantly.

Peter shook his head back and forth on the wall. "You're gonna make me ask, right?"

"Ask what?" she pretended.

"Did you ever date?" exclaimed Peter, as quickly as if removing a bandage.

Sarah contemplated the question. "We dated twice. We both thought we had to try, right? It seemed logical," remembered Sarah. "The first date went pretty well…dinner and a movie kind of thing."

Peter took note of Sarah's pregnant pause.

"The second one was good, too, until…we kissed…that didn't

go too well."

Peter looked on, wondering.

"We both recoiled, like we had tasted bad fish."

"What?! Why?"

Sarah tossed her arms in the air. "We looked at each other, horrified we caused such a reaction. Then, we laughed really hard that we both had the same reaction!" she explained, "We decided that because our relationship started in such a dreadful way, intimacy caused some sort of mental reaction that fed off the horror."

"What happened after that?" asked Peter.

"Once we got that out of the way, we became as close as two people can possibly become without having any sexual attraction for one another."

"You mean like…"

"Sister and brother, yeah."

"Yeah?"

"Yeah."

Peter smiled. He didn't know exactly why, but he did. After a few seconds, he asked, "Sarah?"

"Yes?"

"Are you hungry?"

"Very."

"I know a place nearby."

"I'll trust your judgment."

Peter stood up in the hallway and offered his hand to Sarah, who took it. They turned together and started down the hall. Sarah slowed and asked, "Do you want to change first?"

Peter looked down on his stained clothes. "They're dry," he responded. "Besides, the place is dark."

The two started again, and Peter took Sarah's hand. This time, he stopped and faced her.

"I'm curious," he stated before kissing her.

Neither pulled away. In fact, both deepened the act and mutually continued in earnest. Peter separated slowly without losing eye contact.

"Good?" he requested.

"Very," she replied. "Good?" she also requested.

"Very."

As Sarah Garrity and Peter Max boarded the elevator, he asked, "I called every Marriott within forty miles. They said you weren't checked in. Do you use an alias or something?"

She explained, "I always stay at a competitor's hotel."

The doors closed as the two continued to hold hands, and Peter responded, "How unpredictable."

THE END

www.ingramcontent.com/pod-product-compliance
Lightning Source LLC
Chambersburg PA
CBHW020918140626
46545CB00015B/94